# PRAISE FOR *JESUS > RELIGION*

"A leader has the ability to affect the attitude and beliefs of their followers. Jefferson Bethke is a young leader who has the attention of a passionate generation yearning for truth. This book offers a chance to uncover what an authentic relationship with Jesus looks like. Be prepared for a trip unlike what you'd expect. Buckle up! It will open the eyes of readers of all ages and strengthen the faith of those chasing after the greatest leader this world has ever known."

— Governor Mike Huckabee, syndicated TV and radio host, and *New York Times* best-selling author

"This is a book that will make you think. Jefferson Bethke asks questions that your life really has to answer. Thinkers and seekers and questioners—start here. Wrestle it out. You can't walk away from these provocative pages unmoved."

— Ann Voskamp, author of *New York Times* best-selling book *One Thousand Gifts: A Dare to Live Fully Right Where You Are*

"Jesus is the focal point of the gospel. He is the center and the essence of Christianity. That's why I love Jefferson's wholehearted determination to make Jesus the main thing. As you read his book, you will find yourself challenged to look past prejudice, habits, and traditions and rediscover the person you fell in love with in the first place: Jesus."

— Judah Smith, lead pastor of The City Church and author of *New York Times* best-selling book *Jesus Is _____*.

"Jeff's book will make you stop and listen to a voice in your heart that may have been drowned out by the noise of religion. Listen to that voice, then follow it—right to the feet of Jesus."

— Bob Goff, author of *New York Times* best-selling book *Love Does*

"Leadership is not limited by age. Your legacy is not only determined by what you do as you get old, but also by who you are when you're young. At twenty-three, Jefferson Bethke is leading the way for this next generation of leaders. His raw and fresh approach to faith make this book a must-read for every person looking to discover an authentic relationship with Jesus."

— Brad Lomenick, president of Catalyst
and author of *The Catalyst Leader*

"When Jefferson shares his heart and voice it's simple and it's shocking. It's simple because he presents the truth. It's shocking because we as the Church have added so much to the truth and embraced it as the gospel. He is a voice we need to pay attention to."

— Sheila Walsh, speaker and author
of *God Loves Broken People* and *The
Storm Inside*

"This book helped me to understand and think about the freedom to live in Christ. With biblical principles Jefferson takes us to see Jesus way beyond simply just doctrine and rules."

— Ricardo Kaka, midfielder for Real
Madrid

"Jefferson bridges the gap between Gen X and the Millennials. He doesn't try to rediscover the Bible, but is biblically sound when asking life's big questions and answering them with a fresh approach using today's language and current examples. *Jesus>Religion* is gritty while effortlessly balancing truth and grace. This is the book for the Millennial generation. It should get more views than his YouTube video."

— Candace Cameron Bure, actress and
*New York Times* best-selling author

"The book you hold in your hands is Donald Miller's *Blue Like Jazz* meets C. S. Lewis's *Mere Christianity* meets Augustine's *Confessions*. This book is going to awaken an entire generation to Jesus and His grace."

— Derwin L. Gray, lead pastor of
Transformation Church, author of
*Limitless Life: Breaking Free from the
Labels That Hold You Back*

"Jefferson knows God—flat adores him—fears him—wants to please him more than every human. You feel it every time he talks or writes or does his rap poetry stuff. He sees God and he makes everyone else see him, believe him, and fear him too. I love God more because of his life and I pray that through these words you will too."

—Jennie Allen, author of *Anything*

"Jefferson Bethke is a refreshing voice speaking truth. In his book *Jesus > Religion* he clearly communicates the simplicity of Jesus' message. The book is a must-read for those who are truly interested in understanding who Jesus really is and what his message is all about."

— Craig Gross, author of *Open*, founder of xxxchurch.com

"After viewing his spoken word 'Jesus > Religion' multiple times, I knew Jeff was a Christian that I could easily and readily relate to. The wisdom and knowledge he has of the Bible is a direct correlation to how much he loves Jesus! With great discernment, he wrote this insightful work that has helped shape my knowledge of God's Word, thus directly growing my love for our Creator that much more. It's modern, it's biblically based, and Jeff's testimonies allow readers to easily identify with the goodness of God in their own lives!"

— Landry Fields, small forward for Toronto Raptors

"Christians have tended to have one eye open to sin and the other eye closed to religion. In this book Jefferson talks about the joy of having both eyes open in order to follow Jesus more deeply."

— Pastor Mark Driscoll, founder of Mars Hill Church, the Resurgence, and cofounder of Acts 29

"I'm the sort of person who ought to hate this book. I think *religion* is a good biblical word (James 1:27). And I think the eclipse of the church and distrust of institutions is the primal sin of evangelicalism. But I love this book, and its author, and here's why. Jefferson Bethke turns our attention to Jesus, not as a system or a mascot but as a Person. And he does so with the kind of fresh exuberance that leads us to, not away from, the church. If you're tired of bleached grave religiosity, this effervescent book will give you living Christ renewal."

— Russell D. Moore, president, Ethics and Religious Liberty Commission, Southern Baptist Convention

"In this book, Jefferson Bethke pulls back the curtain on the subtle dangers associated with elevating religion over relationship. Jefferson is blatantly honest and refreshingly authentic as he guides us to the opportunity to leave behind plastic, shallow spirituality and really grasp the life Jesus has for each of us. I've got a feeling this is a book people will be talking about for years."

— Pete Wilson, pastor, author of *Plan B* and *Let Hope In*

"Jeff Bethke in my opinion is a leader for such a time as this. God's hand is clearly on him and I believe he is a voice for his generation. I believe that Jesus has graced him by the Spirit of God to clarify the gospel to people who are un-churched, de-churched, and over-churched. People who need the clutter of Western religiosity removed as it has been hoarding to the point where Jesus cannot be seen, exalted, and treasured. Read *Jesus>Religion* and contemplate the places where falsehood has taken the place of seeing the character of Jesus more clearly."

— Eric Mason, pastor of Epiphany Fellowship, president of Thrive, author of *Manhood Restored*

"Jeff's viral video poem connected with millions of people who feel weighed down by the heavy burden of religious moralism and justification by performance. His new book will take them deeper, as it explores God's grace for sinners through Jesus Christ. Jeff's deeply personal story takes us from the despair of self-righteous religion to the hope, meaning, and grace found in Jesus, and it will resonate with anyone searching for life more abundantly."

— Justin Holcomb, executive director of the Resurgence and pastor at Mars Hill Church

# JESUS>RELIGION

## WHY HE IS SO MUCH BETTER THAN TRYING HARDER, DOING MORE, AND BEING GOOD ENOUGH

## JEFFERSON BETHKE

NELSON
BOOKS

Published in Nashville, Tennessee, by Nelson Books, an imprint of Thomas Nelson. Nelson Books and Thomas Nelson are registered trademarks of HarperCollins Christian Publishing, Inc.

Published in association with Yates & Yates, www.Yates2.com.

Thomas Nelson, Inc., titles may be purchased in bulk for educational, business, fund-raising, or sales promotional use. For information, please e-mail SpecialMarkets@ThomasNelson.com.

Unless otherwise noted, Scripture quotations are taken from THE ENGLISH STANDARD VERSION. © 2001 by Crossway Bibles, a division of Good News Publishers.

Scripture quotations marked MSG are from *The Message* by Eugene H. Peterson. © 1993, 1994, 1995, 1996, 2000. Used by permission of NavPress Publishing Group. All rights reserved.

Scripture quotations marked NIV are from the Holy Bible, New International Version®, NIV®. Copyright © 1973, 1978, 1984, 2011 by Biblica, Inc.™ Used by permission of Zondervan. All rights reserved worldwide. www.zondervan.com.

Page design by Walter Petrie

**Library of Congress Cataloging-in-Publication Data**

Bethke, Jefferson.
  Jesus > religion : why he is so much better than trying harder, doing more, and being good enough / Jefferson Bethke.
    pages cm
  Includes bibliographical references.
  ISBN 978-1-4002-0539-4
  1. Christianity—Essence, genius, nature. 2. Apologetics. 3. Jesus Christ—Person and offices. 4. Christian life. I. Title. II. Title: Jesus greater than religion.
  BT60.B48 2013
  248.4—dc23                                                        2013009395
*Printed in the United States of America*

13 14 15 16 17 RRD 6

*To my wonderful wife, Alyssa—*
*Your grace and encouragement made this book possible.*
*I'm eternally grateful for you!*

# CONTENTS

Author's Note                                                    xi

Foreword                                                        xiii

Introduction: Why I Hate Religion but Love Jesus                xv

1. Will the Real Jesus Please Stand Up?                          1

2. Why I Still Think Jesus Hates Religion                        21
   (and You Should Too)

3. Fundies, Fakes, and Other So-Called Christians                37

4. Religion Makes Enemies / Jesus Makes Friends                  59

5. With Religion, There Are Good and Bad People /                75
   With Jesus, There Are Only Bad People in Need of Grace

6. Religion Is the Means to Get Things from God /                93
   If We Seek Jesus, We Get God

7. With Religion, If You Are Suffering, God Is Punishing You /   113
   God Already Punished Jesus on Your Behalf, So Suffering
   Is His Mercy

8. Religion Says, "God Will Love You If . . ." /    131
   Jesus Says, "God So Loved . . ."

9. Religion Points to a Dim Future /    155
   Jesus Points to a Bright Future

10. Why Jesus Loves the Church (and You Should Too)    181

*Conclusion: Do You Know Jesus?*    199

*Acknowledgments*    203

*Notes*    205

*Recommended Reading*    213

*About the Author*    217

# AUTHOR'S NOTE

This book can be used in a variety of ways. Hopefully you will find it encouraging and it will push you at least a little closer to Jesus. If you'd like to take the conversation further, perhaps you can pull together some friends—maybe from church, school, or where you work—and use the discussion questions at the end of each chapter as a springboard for deeper discussion. Make sure your discussions are guided by gentleness, humility, and learning. We are all on this journey toward real and authentic truth together. You won't find an arbitrary concept when you get there, but a Man with scars in his hands and a crown on his head.

# FOREWORD

*by Lecrae*

As a young man who grew up immersed in music, the party scene, and a culture of self-discovery, I was skeptical of religion. I felt it never quite reached into my world and offered me an interpretation I could understand, let alone accept. I know there are people just like me all over the world waiting for someone to speak our language and give us answers. Jefferson speaks it. It was indigenous voices like his that led me to where I am today. Voices like his inspired me to speak into the culture. There are certain cultural catalysts that spark movements; I've seen it firsthand as I've been graced to play a role in igniting others. Jefferson is no different.

When he first appeared on most of our radars, Jefferson was the poet who articulated profound truths about Jesus and religion. His words connected with people in a revolutionary way. For some, he was articulating exactly what they'd thought but never had the words to say. For others, he was opening their eyes to a new way of seeing Christian faith—one rarely found in popular culture. His words pierced powerfully, because they were a more accurate perception of what it means to follow Jesus and not merely follow rules.

This book is his gift to all who have come to Jefferson's beautiful conclusions and to those who are searching.

His passion for Jesus comes from a masterful collage of pain, darkness, failure, joy, peace, and resolve. He weaves his own life story with weighty truths that will strengthen our hope and give answers where we thought there were none. His writings will encourage, educate, and inspire you to see Jesus as more than a man who followed all the rules and demands that you do likewise. You will be asked to see Jesus as your ultimate hope and satisfaction in this world and the world to come. You will be asked to see Jesus for all that He is.

# INTRODUCTION

*Why I Hate Religion but Love Jesus*

*What if I told you Jesus came to abolish religion?*

*What if I told you getting you to vote Republican really wasn't his mission?*

*What if I told you religious right doesn't automatically mean Christian?*

*And just because you call some people blind, doesn't automatically give you vision.*

*I mean, if religion is so great, why has it started so many wars?*

*Why does it build huge churches, but fail to feed the poor?*

*Tell single moms God doesn't love them, if they've ever had a divorce?*

*Yet God in the Old Testament actually calls the religious people whores.*

A little sharp, I know. When I first wrote those lines, I didn't think so, but when in less than forty-eight hours almost seven million people heard me say those words on YouTube, I realized they resonated with more than just a few people.

My best friend makes professional videos, and we thought it would be fun to shoot a spoken-word poem I had written. To our surprise it went viral overnight. At first I was excited. I was now in the blessed company of "David After the Dentist" and "Charlie Bit My Finger." Then there was panic.

The number of e-mails, messages, and requests became almost unbearable. For about a solid week, everywhere I looked, I was there: *Wall Street Journal, Huffington Post, Yahoo News, Washington Post, New York Times, CBS Morning Show, Glenn Beck*, and others either interviewed me or had a significant piece highlighting the video. One of the YouTube staff even mentioned that something this serious or this explicit about Jesus hardly ever goes viral. In fact #jesushatesreligion was even trending on Twitter for a while. Immediately e-mails started to come in:

> Hello, Jeff. My name is Laura. I just wanted to say thank you sooo much for your videos. I have struggled with drugs, sex, and suicide. I always thought that I wasn't good enough and didn't belong anywhere ever since I was raped when I was seven. I knew God growing up, but I thought he was just some mythical figure everyone worshiped. One day I was fed up with all of it and decided that was

all I could take—I was going to kill myself after school. All day I went through my head saying, It's finally going to be done, I don't have to worry. On my way home I got on Facebook one last time and my friend had posted your video "Why I Hate Religion, but Love Jesus." I figured I might as well watch it because I'm going to end it all any way. I immediately started crying because the video made me realize that it's okay that I'm not perfect. There is a place where I belong. Your video gave me the courage to move on and say that I can make it through life. You are my biggest role model . . . besides God. lol When I get so low that I can't think straight, I just watch your videos over and over. They bring me peace in my mind that God still loves me even if I've screwed up.

And another:

As I moved away to college, I also moved away from the church, attempting to find my own path. When I stumbled upon your video, I was lost after being disowned by my family for moving away from the Catholic faith. Watching it opened my eyes to Jesus again and made me realize that Jesus isn't what I grew up with everyday in the church but rather loving and pouring with grace. I started going to the Christian services located on my campus and got back on the right track in life, learning that no matter what anyone else would say about my past, present, or future sins that God will still love me and Jesus is truly everything.

E-mails like these flooded in by the hundreds. What had I said in my video that struck such a chord? Why were these people sharing these things with me? To be honest, I was overwhelmed at first. I'm not a counselor. I'm not a pastor. I'm a messed-up twenty-three-year-old who just graduated from college. I was being messaged, e-mailed, and tweeted by thousands of people who were sharing their raw testimonies with me, a complete stranger. Many even stated that it was the first time they had shared their secrets with anyone. I was wondering, *What did I say? What was it about the poem that was so different? Isn't this just the good news of Jesus that's been preached for the last two thousand years?*

I realized the e-mails were showing just how right the original poem that sparked it all in the first place was. Many people had been sold religion with a nice Jesus sticker slapped on it. Many people had been burned by so-called Christians. Many people had been abused, hurt, mistreated, and maligned all in the name of the Father, the Son, and the Holy Spirit. But what their souls were craving was the true Jesus. The One who heals. The One who redeems. The One who gives life.

Let me be straight with you: I'm not really qualified to write this book. I don't have a Bible or seminary degree. I'm not a pastor or a counselor. I don't know biblical languages and don't know how to do exegesis—whatever that even is. Again,

I'm just a messed-up twenty-three-year-old guy. But I know that God has quite the sense of humor. It only takes a quick peek into Christian history to realize I'm almost the exact type of person he is looking for. A wise man two thousand years ago put it this way: "But God chose what is foolish in the world to shame the wise; God chose what is weak in the world to shame the strong."[1] Paul tells us that God loves using people who are useless by worldly standards—because then he gets all the credit. A crooked stick can still draw a straight line, and a messed-up dude like me can still write about an awesome God. I've tasted grace and can't help but tell others about it.

My hope in sharing my story is that it would somehow thread itself into yours, ultimately weaving us both closer to the ultimate story of a God in heaven who pursues and loves people like us.

# CHAPTER 1

# WILL THE REAL JESUS PLEASE STAND UP?

What do you believe?

No, really. What do you *really* believe? I'm not talking about what you put on your Facebook profile or what box you check on an application. What do you put your faith in? What drives you? What's your identity? I'm sure we all have some canned answers to those questions, but when it gets down to it, we know that's a load of crap.

If you are anything like me, you probably grew up thinking there was a God—whatever that means, right? Soon enough reality started to clash with this idea, and the idea of a real God seemed to become more distant. I still held on to the Christian tagline simply for identity purposes, but once I got to high school, it all seemed pretty ridiculous. There really was no need for him. Sure I could still call myself a Christian, but only when it seemed to benefit me. Other than that, I didn't want him anymore.

My true religion, as it is with most of my American peers, was the religion of moralism dressed in Christian clothes. I believed there was a god out there somewhere, that he wants us to be good kids, and that if we are, he tells us how much he loves us, puts our pictures on the fridge, and gives us a trophy—because everyone's a winner, right?

I was a Christian by default. Everyone else said they were Christians; my mom took me to church; there was a Bible in the house. So I thought all that made me a Christian too. Saying I was a Christian seemed to get me further with my friends, family, and society than saying I was not. Being a Christian made life easier for me. But I didn't actually love or serve Jesus.

Isn't that the story for many of us in America? Christianity is our default setting. We say we're Christians because it seems nice, makes us look moral, keeps the parents off our backs, and keeps us out of hell—*that is, if we even believe in hell.*

My mom and I went to church enough to know the rituals and songs, but I never felt like a "church kid." I heard enough sermons to know Jesus died for me, but I also had such a broken and painful life that I figured Jesus wasn't relevant. My parents never got married, so I grew up with just my mom. She is an amazing woman who did everything in her power to give me every opportunity possible. However, a physical handicap and mental struggles made it so she was unable to work very often. This meant Section Eight housing, welfare, social security, and food stamps. We moved around a lot—I went to eight schools from kindergarten through high school—and didn't live in the nicest areas.

I remember going to church and enjoying the games, the felt board, and the songs; but it always felt so disconnected. All the other kids seemed to have it together, and I never felt completely comfortable in that crowd. So I decided to fake it. I figured that if I could out-good the good kids, then I'd fit in. If little Johnny got a gold star, then I'd make sure to get a platinum one.

I became prideful and religious. This attitude festered and solidified itself in me all the way into my teenage years. When I got to high school, I thought I was good because I didn't smoke, drink, or have sex. I constantly thought I was better than all *those* people. I had just enough church to think that I could be good enough for God. I had just enough Jesus not to need him at all.

The funny part is that—even though I thought I was—I really wasn't a good kid. Starting in middle school, I was a troublemaker. I had a careless attitude toward school, my mom, and my life. I had bad grades, got kicked out of school for fighting and stealing, and developed a porn addiction that lasted more than eight years.

High school began, and things only got worse. I didn't even attempt to turn in any of my assignments, and so I flunked out my freshman year. I went to school just to keep in touch with friends and talk to girls. My mom knew my friends weren't good influences, and so we moved—again—to another town about thirty minutes away.

To some degree this was an awesome fresh start. I immediately got plugged in with the "good" kids who didn't party or drink, and I loved them. I also loved baseball and made it onto the school team. My life was baseball and my friends—it was looking good.

Then, my junior year of high school, my mom told me what was devastating news at the time. She came into my room, sat me down, and told me she was gay. She went on to include that she had fought it all her life and that the woman whom she had invited to live with us months earlier under the pretense that she was just a friend who needed help was actually her partner. (She fessed up after a fight between them.)

I felt betrayed by my mom, embarrassed for not figuring out why another woman lived in our house, and ashamed that my mom was gay. What would my friends think? My attitude was so self-centered back then. All I could think about was myself. I was a good Christian kid, so I couldn't have a gay mom, right?

After that, my mom threw in the towel on the traditional Christian faith. The treatment of gays by conservative Christians finally got to her. My initial thought was, *Well, if Jesus didn't work for her, why would he work for me?* So I gave up on God too. I was in pain. I was lonely. I wanted to escape but couldn't. I went from religion to rebellion. I figured if it felt

4

good, I should do it. I worshiped girls, relationships, and my reputation. If getting more girls and drinking more beer meant I'd be "cool," then why not? But I soon discovered that lifestyle was like drinking saltwater. If you are extremely thirsty, you'll settle for it, but it just makes you thirstier. Every girl eventually became tiresome, and it was on to the next one.

On top of all this, I began to resent my mom. I despised her. Bitterness grew heavy. We lived in the same house but rarely spoke. I partied even harder and cared even less. I stopped looking for the right girl and started looking for an easy girl. I had the world's idea of pleasure at my fingertips, but something deep inside kept gnawing at me. Most of the time I was going too fast to notice it. It was only those few minutes before I'd fall asleep at night that my soul would be quiet enough to tell me what I was doing wasn't working.

I hear a lot of people say that the fear of death and the fear of public speaking are two of the main fears in my generation, but I disagree. I think it's the fear of silence. We refuse to turn off our computers, turn off our phones, log off Facebook, and just sit in silence, because in those moments we might actually have to face up to who we really are. We fear silence like it's an invisible monster, gnawing at us, ripping us open, and showing us our dissatisfaction. Silence is *terrifying*.

Then I graduated, had a fun summer, and headed off to a Christian college. In San Diego. Completely on my own. I didn't go because the school was Christian. I went because they had an awesome baseball team and a beautiful field. The campus—and baseball field—is literally on the beach; you can almost hit a home run into the water. It's no surprise that within the first semester, I got put on academic probation, cut from the baseball team, and dumped by my first serious girlfriend. Because baseball and girls were my life, I felt I had lost everything important. It was devastating, and for the first time in my life, I wasn't "good enough." I was broken.

Initially I blamed God for the pain in my life, but slowly I started to hear the whisper of his grace. I didn't know it then, but God broke me to fix me because he loved me. Author C. S. Lewis said, "God whispers to us in our pleasures, speaks in our conscience, but shouts in our pains: It is His megaphone to rouse a deaf world."[1]

Because of this, I was finally ready to listen. It was a messy process, however.

Looking back, I can't pinpoint one day when it all seemed to click. It was more like a period of three to four months when I stood at arm's length with Jesus. I really had nothing to lose, but this whole grace thing didn't make much sense to me. My mom said I was the annoying kid who always asked "why" after everything. (I pray to Jesus this particular character trait doesn't get passed down to my future kids.) I am still like that to this day, and it played out when I finally started to get drawn in by grace. I had to investigate. I had to have the answers. I had to know if grace was real.

I still remember going to the college library one day and asking how many books a student could check out at one time. The answer was fifteen, so I went back to my dorm room with fifteen books on Jesus, Christianity, and apologetics. Through some of those authors, God's grace slowly melted the crust off my heart. I started to see an enormous difference in the Christianity I thought I knew and the Christianity proclaimed in the New Testament. I finally started to see:

The Bible isn't a rule book. It's a love letter.
I'm not an employee. I'm a child.
It's not about my performance. It's about Jesus'
performance for me.

Grace isn't there for some future me but for the real me. The me who struggled. The me who was messy. The me who was addicted to porn. The me who didn't have all the answers. The me who was insecure. He loved me in my mess; he was not waiting until I cleaned myself up. That truth changed my life, and I'm convinced it can change yours.

## FINDING THE REAL JESUS

After my head-on collision with grace, I couldn't get enough of Jesus. It wasn't that everything difficult disappeared, but I now felt an anchor amid the pain. Being a new Christian, however, I didn't know what to do, how to act, what Bible studies to go to, or what CDs to listen to. I had a lot of friends, but not many of them were Christians. The first six months of my new life with Jesus, I was alone and guessing how to "do" the Christian faith. I spent a lot of nights in my dorm room reading my Bible—which was better than going out and partying like I did the semester before.

Though I didn't have many Christian friends, I was at a Christian university. So I decided to copy what "being a Christian" was all about by watching others. I took off my earrings, stopped wearing basketball jerseys, tried my hardest to memorize Hillsong United's greatest hits, and listened to the Christian radio station. I thought that if I did enough Christian things, it would bring peace to my life. It didn't work.

Six months in, I had done everything I thought I should be doing as a Christian, but I still had desires I thought were supposed to disappear—lust, pride, and pleasure. Wasn't Jesus supposed to make my life better? I had been duped. My "Christianity" was once again just the American religion of work hard, do good, feel good, and maybe God will say, "We good."

I realized I was following the wrong Jesus—not that there is a "wrong" Jesus—but I was following a fake version of the real one. This realization came to me as I listened to a Christian radio station one day. During a commercial break, they did a fifteen-second spot about the station that consisted of kids laughing, happy music, and the slogan, "Music you can trust, because it's safe for the whole family!"

I remember thinking, *Safe for the whole family? Is Jesus really safe for the whole family?*

I realized we had created a Jesus who's safe for the whole family. But if we were honest, we'd ask, how is a homeless dude who was murdered on a cross for saying he was God safe for the whole family? Not to mention that Paul told us if we choose to follow his example as a follower of Jesus, we will be treated the way that he was.[2]

We've lost the real Jesus—or at least exchanged him for a newer, safer, sanitized, ineffectual one. We've created a Christian subculture that comes with its own set of customs, rules, rituals, paradigms, and products that are nowhere near the rugged, revolutionary faith of biblical Christianity. In our subculture Jesus would have never been crucified— he's too nice.

We claim Jesus is our homeboy, but sometimes we look more like the people Jesus railed against. The same scathing indictments Jesus brought against the religious leaders of his day—the scribes and Pharisees—he could bring down on many of America's Christian leaders.[3] No wonder the world hates us. Most of the time we're persecuted not because we love Jesus, but because we're prideful, arrogant jerks who don't love the real Jesus. We're often judgmental, hypocritical, and legalistic while claiming to follow a Jesus who is forgiving, authentic, and loving.

Sometimes people will hate us because we preach the same gospel Jesus preached, and sometimes people will hate us because we're jerks. Let's not do the second one and blame it on the first. If we honestly reflected on Scripture and the state of

American Christianity today, we'd be hard-pressed to say we haven't exchanged the real Jesus for one of our own invention.

God didn't create us to work at the food bank once a year and feel good about ourselves. He didn't create us to say looking at porn only once a month is a victory. He didn't create us to walk by a homeless guy begging for money and think, *He'll probably just buy some beer.* God didn't create us to come to him only when we need him—like he's our eternal dentist or something.

The Jesus of the Bible is a radical man with a radical message, changing people's lives in a radical way. In the Scriptures, Jesus isn't safe. No one knew what to do with him. The liberals called him too conservative, and the conservatives called him too liberal. I mean, think about it: His first miracle was turning water into wine. He made a whip of leather and went UFC on people who'd pimped out his father's temple. He completely disregarded any social, gender, or racial boundary his society imposed. He called himself the Son of God. He called himself the judge over everyone, determining who goes to heaven and hell. He said things like, "Unless you eat the flesh of the Son of Man and drink his blood, you have no life in you."[4] That's dangerous—and weird.

I don't care what church you grew up in, that sounds less like the Jesus we think we know and more like Hannibal Lecter. Jesus also forgives sins, which is dangerous because only God can forgive sins, yet the religious people claimed Jesus was just a man.[5]

But we don't like a dangerous Jesus because a dangerous Jesus isn't a profitable Jesus. So, we've made a safe Jesus:

We don't celebrate the gift of Jesus on Christmas. We celebrate the gifts we get.

We don't celebrate his triumphant resurrection and victory over Satan, sin, and death on Easter. We talk about the brunch.

We don't call Jesus God. We call him good.

We don't tell people they're sinners in need of a savior, because they might stop coming—and giving—to church.

In many ways, Christianity has become all about those green pieces of paper with dead presidents on them. In 2010 Americans spent a little over $135 billion on Christmas and another $13 billion on Easter.[6] Who would have thought a little baby born in a filthy animal barn some two thousand years ago would be such a great excuse to feed our material addictions?

We have branded Jesus beyond recognition. Church has become a business. Jesus is our marketing scheme. We create bookstores, T-shirts, bracelets, bumper stickers, and board games all in the name of Jesus. In 2007 some woman even made national news for selling a pancake with Jesus' face on it on eBay.[7]

Now don't get me wrong. There's a degree to which that

11

stuff is okay. I mean, chances are you bought the book you're reading right now. I know I buy my fair share of Christian books—in fact, my wife says I buy too many, and I'm going to make us broke. But questions continue coming back to me: Are we really getting it? Have we made that stuff more important than Jesus? How come American Christianity is so different from the Bible's vibrant, uncontrollable, and unpredictable Christianity?

The reason we aren't fulfilled or satisfied by our version of Christianity is because it *isn't* Christianity.

> We have religion, but we don't have Jesus.
> We have a good role model, but we don't have God.
> We have theological debates, but we don't have the living Word.
> We have good works, but we don't have the source of good works.
> We have love, but not the God who is love.

We have completely neutered grace (my good works save me, but we still call it grace), made God a math equation (God will like me if I'm good), and turned Jesus into Mr. Rogers ("Howdy, neighbor"). But Jesus isn't rocking a cardigan, and he doesn't talk softly through his nose. He's a roaring lion.

In author C. S. Lewis's classic book *The Lion, the Witch and the Wardrobe*, the kids ask if the lion, Aslan—who represents Jesus—is safe. "'Safe?' said Mr. Beaver; 'don't you hear what

Mrs. Beaver tells you? Who said anything about safe? 'Course he isn't safe. But he's good. He's the King, I tell you.'"[8]

That's what the real Jesus is like. He isn't safe. His words, his life, and his cross completely destroy the notion of him being safe. His grace is dangerous, ferocious, violent, and uncontrollable. It can't be tamed. Does it bother anyone else that seemingly the first, and sometimes only, prayer people pray when they go on mission trips is that they'd stay "safe"?

It's important that we discover the real Jesus by seeing what the Bible says about him. I think you might be as surprised as I was.

## NOT YOUR MOM'S JESUS

Looking back on my time in Sunday school and Christian summer camp, I remember two verses that were often shared to encourage us kids:

> But they who wait for the LORD shall renew their strength;
> they shall mount up with wings like eagles;
> they shall run and not be weary;
> they shall walk and not faint.

And,

> For I know the plans I have for you, declares the Lord, plans
> for welfare and not for evil, to give you a future and a hope.[9]

These verses say that God has a beautiful plan for our lives, that we're precious and unique snowflakes, and that when we wait on him, he'll raise us up on wings of eagles.

Are these verses true? Yes. But not in the way we might think. God does have a great plan for our lives, but it probably isn't *our* plan. In the early years of Christianity, most Christians were enemies of the state, and some were used as food for the animals in the Roman gladiator games. So next time you quote those verses, remind yourself that they were just as true for the people having their flesh ripped apart by lions as they are for you. Would you be down with God if that was his plan for your welfare?

Looking back, though, I realize I'd completely prostituted those verses and made them fit my feel-good Christianity. Surely God disciplining me or putting me through trials wouldn't be his "good plan" for my life! It must be from the devil, right? The truth is, sometimes the good plan he has for our lives is to make us look more like him, which more often than not takes pain. But we don't use the verses in that context. We'd rather just put them on T-shirts and bumper stickers.

Just once, I'd like to see a T-shirt that reads—even if it doesn't all fit on the front—"From his mouth comes a sharp sword with which to strike down the nations, and he will rule them with a rod of iron. He will tread the winepress of the fury of God the Almighty. On his robe and on his thigh he has a name written, King of kings and Lord of lords."[10]

But we don't like that verse. It's dangerous and doesn't fit with our modern view of God. Yet that verse is just as true as the ones we put on our bookmarks. When Jesus comes back the second time, he isn't coming to sprinkle love dust on everyone. He's coming to make war on sin and rebellion.

Do you believe in *that* Jesus?

Once I began to realize the packaged Christianity I grew up with didn't tell the whole story, I began to see this dangerous Jesus everywhere in Scripture. I would come across passages that completely confronted my sanitized Christianity.

Jesus was homeless?

Jesus called people sons of the devil?

Jesus actually told his disciples they needed to physically follow him, not just sign a card and raise their hands?

Jesus told people they couldn't be a follower of him until they took up the most brutal torture device ever invented, the cross?[11]

One of my favorite verses can be found in the book of Isaiah: "All of us have become like one who is unclean, and all our righteous acts are like filthy rags."[12] We often miss that our "righteous acts" are "filthy" before God. Not just our bad days, but our extremely good days too! Praying, reading the Bible, giving to the poor, and going to church nine times a week? Filthy rags apart from Jesus and his cross. Tell me that isn't just a little bit controversial.

15

And if that God isn't shocking enough for you, author Francis Chan shares in his book *Crazy Love* that the Hebrew word for "filthy rags" can be interpreted as "menstrual garments."[13] In that verse God says our good works are no better than a bloody tampon. Next time you're in a public restroom and you see the waste can, feel free to remind yourself that's your righteousness apart from Jesus. (Gross, I know.)

This abrasive message wasn't just from God the Father either. Jesus delivered his fair share of one-liners to the most religiously zealous of his day—"hypocrites," "brood of vipers," and "murderers."[14] Would this Jesus get kicked out of your church or criticized on your blog for not being gracious or kind enough?

And don't you find it interesting that some of Jesus' harshest words were reserved for the most devout religious people of his day? You would think he would condemn the bad sins of marginalized people of society such as prostitutes, drug dealers, and tax collectors, right? Instead, speaking to the religious leaders, he said stuff like, "Truly, I say to you, the tax collectors and the prostitutes go into the kingdom of God before you. For John [the Baptist] came to you in the way of righteousness, and you did not believe him, but the tax collectors and the prostitutes believed him."[15]

If that won't make a religious person faint, I don't know what will.

Jesus hung out with the most marginalized and disrespected people of society, and he was fiercely opposed to anyone representing him in a hypocritical way. His words should not only shock us but also make us fear, because they were written just as much to us Christians today as they were to the religious leaders of his day, the Pharisees.

I certainly have focused on outward appearance and made extra to-do lists to add to my salvation, all while neglecting the simple needs of others. I'm often more Pharisee than saint. I'd rather people tell me how awesome I am than how awesome Jesus is. I'd rather concentrate on other people's sins before I look at my own. More often than not, I sense the toxic Pharisee spirit rising up within me.

## THE REAL THING

Do you ever have internal arguments with yourself? When you know something is wrong but you can't seem to beat it? That's me when I have a self-righteous or legalistic attitude. Sometimes I hate the way I treat people. I often get bothered by how words come out of my mouth. I occasionally even get depressed when I read the New Testament because I read the stories of the Pharisees and humbly have to admit I act more like them sometimes even though I *want* to be more like Jesus.

Whenever I'm stuck in a rut, it is Jesus' sharp words that wake me up. There's something about the tone and force of Jesus' words that shocks me back into reality. It's important to understand that Jesus never says something without a purpose. He desires everyone to come to repentance, and if he speaks harshly, it's so that we'll come to know the real thing. Sometimes soft words don't penetrate, don't cut, don't wake us up. In the same way we need a hard shovel to break up hard soil, Jesus sometimes has to use hard words to break up hard hearts. He does it in hopes of bringing us to joy.

I think Jesus was using those harsh statements to say that we've traded in the real thing for things that don't matter. We've completely missed what God is after, what he's doing, and how to relate to him. He made it very clear that he's not after our external behaviors but instead after our hearts.[16] He doesn't want what you *do*. He just wants *you*. Have you ever sat in that? Have you ever had a moment where that sank in?

Jesus is so much greater than "don't smoke, don't drink, and don't have sex." As Christians, we need to stop forcing the Bible into our own judgments and instead humbly and prayerfully open our minds in hopes that God might reveal himself deeply. It's a dangerous and scary proposition for sure, but there is so much freedom and life in no longer defending or molding Jesus to our own liking, and just letting him be who he says he is—a cultural iconoclast who makes it difficult for any of us to put him in our nice, cute, and tidy "Christian" box.

When I was trying to earn Jesus by being good, I missed the real Jesus who wants us to love him and serve him not for what he gives but for who he is—dangerous, unpredictable, radical, and amazing.

1. Jeff opens his book by saying, "My true religion, as it is with most of my American peers, was just moralism dressed in Christian clothes." What do you think he means by that? Where do you see things in your life where you might see this?

2. How has Christianity been the default option for you in your life?

3. After his mom's news about her sexuality, Jeff gave up on God and rebelled. He likens this rebellion to drinking saltwater. Have you ever tried to quench a thirst but realized you were at the wrong source? If so, describe what happened.

4. Why is the fear of silence the greatest fear for many in our culture, especially young adults?

5. Have you ever interpreted the Bible as a love letter? Why or why not?

6. Soon after he began to follow Jesus, Jeff realized he had been duped into following a safe, ineffectual Jesus—a Jesus of his own making—rather than the real one. Describe the real Jesus.

7. Jeff states that Christianity has become a financial industry. In what ways have you experienced this? Have you ever experienced Christianity rising above a consumer-driven culture?

8. Have you been resistant to believing God's plan might include discipline for your life? How might God use trials to help you become more like Jesus?

9. Why do Christians focus more on supposed acts of righteousness than the needs of others?

# CHAPTER 2

# WHY I STILL THINK JESUS HATES RELIGION (AND YOU SHOULD TOO)

It was that time of the year when you could feel a mixture of intense emotions in the air—the joy of the semester almost being done, along with the pressure of having to pass through final exams first. People were stressed. The campus was fairly quiet as students were trying to make up for all the studying they didn't do the previous three and a half months. I had come to expect a few breaks that included fun treats or programs during finals week that the student life department at my previous self-proclaimed Christian college make available. Sometimes there were free massages in the student lounge. Sometimes there was free food or candy.

Even though I had just transferred to a secular liberal arts university, I expected the same. While I was in my room studying—most likely Facebooking, but let's not talk about that—I heard a knock at the door. I answered it to be greeted by my lovely RA (resident assistant) who was holding a bucket of lollipops in one hand and a bucket of condoms in the other.

She cheerfully said, "Candies and condoms! Be safe and have a stress-free finals week!"

I remember thinking, *Just what I needed to help me study for finals—high fructose corn syrup and latex birth control.*

I definitely wasn't at a Christian college anymore! Later that year they did something similar, where they taped "sex facts" and condoms to the walls of the dorm. I think they used to use staples, but as you can imagine, *it wasn't very effective.*

Talk about a quick change. It didn't take me more than a few hours to see the glaring difference between my strict Christian college in San Diego and my new liberal arts university in Portland. Whatever comes to mind when you think of Portland, that is exactly the essence of this school. It was the mecca of gay rights. They banned bottled water because it wasn't environmentally friendly. Everyone had dreads, and none of the girls shaved their armpit hair. Well, that last one is not *completely true.* It was the type of university that had used books by Richard Dawkins and Christopher Hitchens as textbooks and dripped with a granola-liberal-progressive spirit. But I loved it. Really. I absolutely loved it. If I had to do it all over again, I would have gone there in the first place.

Now, what's really funny is while I was at the Christian school, I wasn't a Christian. But while I was at the secular school, I was a Christian. You'd think I would have wanted to go back to the Christian school, right? It was the opposite. I found the Christian school to be stuffy, hypocritical, and judgmental. I could no longer stand praying after baseball practice with thirty guys who wore crosses around their necks, knowing a few hours later they'd have a beer in one hand and a girl in the other (myself included). Weirdly, my new university felt accepting and loving. There was no guessing if someone was really a Christian or not. If you said you were a Christian at that school, it wasn't to gain you any points—in fact, you probably lost some. There was something about that type of atmosphere that drew me in.

My senior year I was an RA—which pretty much means I was the dorm's "dad." I was the guy who would let you in if you locked yourself out, wrote you up if you broke the rules— there weren't many—and would be there if you were having emotional or academic problems. Dealing with students daily, I got a pulse on the common conceptions they held toward God, Jesus, religion, and Christians.

What constantly surprised me was the ignorance of most college students regarding Jesus. I heard things such as, "I could never follow Jesus; I still want to drink beer." Or, "Why would I like Jesus? He hates gays." I remember thinking, *Huh?*

*I still drink beer, and I don't hate gays.* My favorite was one of my baseball teammate's responses after I asked him what he thought about Jesus: "Yeah, I love Jesus—and Buddha too. I'm a Christian Buddhist." It took everything in me not to laugh. Christian Buddhist? That's like saying you're a lactose-intolerant cheese lover.

A college campus is an interesting place. Students have little to no responsibility, question everything they believe in, and live within one hundred feet of all their friends. There's also a huge dark side to most colleges. As an RA I had a front-row view of the pain in my generation. Colleges these days are breeding grounds for poor decisions, emotional brokenness, and sharp pain.

This is all behind the scenes, of course, because the girl who was raped freshman year and the guy who hates himself and struggles with depression don't seem broken when sitting in a lecture hall debate. People don't flaunt their brokenness when trying to prove themselves. But in their dorm rooms in the middle of the night after another disaster or one-too-many shots, I got to see people become transparent over and over again. They'd continually admit their lives weren't working. They were empty. Longing. Desiring. Searching.

One friend's sister had just admitted she was gay to the family, and it was tearing them apart because their dad refused to "have a gay daughter." Another friend admitted she hated herself for losing her virginity to her ex-boyfriend, whom she didn't even speak to anymore. Another felt the immense pressure of balancing school and child care because she was caring for her little sister now that her dad had left and her mom had to work.

I saw some of my peers nearly drink themselves to death or try to kill themselves—and without the ambulances showing up so fast, they just might have.

I wondered, *How am I any different?* Just two years before, I had struggled with depression. I had struggled with suicidal thoughts. I had struggled with the guilt and shame that so often come with recreational dating. I had spent the first year of college shotgunning beers, messing around with girls, acting like the world existed to cater to my needs, and never taking a second to pull out the emotional, spiritual, and mental shrapnel that had been lodged in my soul by the "me" lifestyle. Inside I was just a scared little boy who had been deeply insecure his whole life and lived in hopes that others would tell me I was good enough.

Of course, none of us would admit it so plainly, and for nineteen years of my life, I wouldn't have either, but isn't it true? Why else do we do most of the things we do? My generation is the most fatherless and insecure generation that's ever lived, and we are willing to sacrifice everything if we just can be told we are loved.

*If only we knew just how loved we really are.*

So being a follower of Jesus now, and knowing just how gracious he had been to restore me, heal me, and pursue me,

I longed so deeply to share his love with these students. Over and over again, though, I'd get the same response whenever I'd bring up Jesus. Literally, the overall essence of Jesus to these students had been boiled down to whether or not someone could say the *f* word. Immediately, they'd bring up periphery issues that Jesus barely mentions as their biggest opposition to him. Ironically, the reasons they opposed Jesus were sometimes the reasons Jesus opposed the religious people of his day. Half the time, they weren't even rejecting Jesus; they were rejecting what he rejected!

I sat in bed one night and wondered, *When on earth did "hates gays, can't drink beer, and no tattoos" become the essence of Christianity?* It hit me that my friends weren't the ones to blame for their confusion. They had gotten this idea from people they grew up with, churches they went to as kids, or preachers they saw on TV. It was the church's fault that they thought this was what real Christianity was all about. As I've heard said, "Of 100 unsaved men, one might read the Bible, but the other 99 will read the Christian."[1]

Ouch.

I'm sure we'd have a very different Bible if it were written simply by observing modern-day Christians.

My peers couldn't separate Jesus from religion because they weren't reading the Bible to learn about Jesus; they were looking to the Christian religion to understand him. What they were rebelling against was *religion*. People lamented that they had tried Christianity, and it didn't work. But last time

I checked, you don't *try* Christianity; either your heart has been transformed by Jesus or it hasn't.

> But you can *try* religion.
> You can *try* to follow the rules.
> You can *try* to climb up to heaven.

But all you'll do is white-knuckle your way to religious despair. It won't work. It never does.

That's when I started to notice an interesting trend: When I juxtaposed religion and Jesus in my conversations, they took a different turn. It allowed people to pull back a little and see him in a different light. They no longer were just brushing him off, but were actually pursuing, thinking, and investigating the man named Jesus. And that's when I started to write the poem "Why I Hate Religion but Love Jesus."

## SAYING NOTHING NEW

Some of you may be thinking, *Wait a minute: you can't hate religion and love Jesus. Jesus IS a religion.* To which I'd answer yes and no. If you mean by religion, "a set of beliefs concerning the cause, nature, and purpose of the universe," then yes and amen, Christianity is a religion. But by that definition, *so is atheism.* But if we mean by religion, "what one must do, or behave like, in order to gain right standing with God," then real Christianity isn't a religion.

I had been a Christian for about a year when I realized Jesus isn't just one of many saviors. Following him is fundamentally different from practicing other world religions. There was something almost upside-down or antithetical to him.

All the other religions center on people's righteousness—what we do and how good we are. Real Christianity centers on Jesus' righteousness—what he has done and how good he is.

All the other religions essentially say, "This is what you have to do to be in right standing with God." Jesus comes to earth and says, "This is what I've freely done for you to put you in right standing with God."

Religion says do. Jesus says done.

Religion is man searching for God. Jesus is God
  searching for man.

Religion is pursuing God *by* our moral efforts. Jesus
  is God pursuing us *despite* our moral efforts.

Religious people *kill* for what they believe. Jesus
  followers *die* for what they believe.

That's when it hit me: No wonder Christianity and Jesus' message of salvation is called *good news*. It isn't just good advice (religion); it's good news (Jesus). It's not declaring what we must do, but declaring what he has already done. It's almost as if Jesus is the eternal paperboy delivering a newspaper declaring something that has *already* happened. The only question with Jesus is, will we follow him?

Now, a lot of people might fire back, saying, "Jesus didn't come to abolish religion. He even said he came to fulfill it." Well, not quite. He said, "Do not think that I have come to abolish the Law or the Prophets; I have not come to abolish them but to fulfill them. For truly, I say to you, until heaven and earth pass away, not an iota, not a dot, will pass from the Law until all is accomplished."[2]

When I read that, I say amen. Jesus isn't talking about religion; he's talking about the law.

Jesus wants to make it clear: he isn't taking God's moral law lightly. The only difference is, he didn't come to crush us with it—which religious people do, like the leaders in John 8—but rather, he came to fulfill it *for* us. When something is "fulfilled," it means it has reached its end or completion. That's what Jesus said he was doing. He was fulfilling the righteous requirements of it, on our behalf, to give us perfect standing with God.

For example, at the time of writing this, I'm getting married in a couple of weeks. Once Alyssa and I are married we will no longer be engaged. We fulfilled that requirement, which suited us well for the time between dating and getting married. We, however, are moving on to something *better.* That's what Jesus was saying here. It's not like he is abolishing the law. It was there for a reason. It had a purpose. The Old Testament law's role was put in place to show us how God aligned the universe to work, and also to show us we couldn't live up to his standard.

It's scandalous to say, but one of the uses of the law was to show us we couldn't fully keep it and needed a savior. It was—and still is—a mirror to show us where we need Jesus. Even the animal sacrifices mandated in the law to the Israelites were there to show them they *needed* a substitute. They couldn't do it on their own, and ultimately Jesus fulfilled that requirement.

So Jesus came and fulfilled the requirements of it to satisfy God. He lived it perfectly. And then instead of the Old Testament law becoming our standard or law, Jesus himself became our law. He gave us his perfect standing by fulfilling God's righteous requirements and then on the cross took all our sin, failure, guilt, and shame. A pretty sweet exchange, if you ask me. And now we no longer solely live up to an external code, but rather live in relationship with a person who then shows us how to properly view that code. Jesus became the face of the Law rather than the concrete tablets Moses is always holding in those ancient depictions.

Love is the new law.

The way I think about it is this: if I'm ever tempted to cheat on Alyssa, I could motivate myself by the law—I won't cheat on her because I might go to hell, etc.—or I could motivate myself with love—I don't want to cheat on her because she is *better* than anything out there. So it is with us and God. Jesus ushered in a more beautiful covenant. One that is perfected in love, not in hateful and fearful obedience.

The law was just a foretaste of Jesus. To know all the shadows and pictures in the Old Testament were simply a picture of him is astounding. Sacrificing a goat seems a little weird and disgusting until you see it actually had a reason. The sacrificial system was God's way of saying sin breeds death. Someone must die when there is sin.

All the mandates and requirements God laid out for the Israelites were ultimately mini arrows pointing to Jesus. The lamb the Israelites needed to sacrifice for sin was God's way of saying, "There is one coming after you who will not only be a picture of sacrifice and forgiveness like these lambs, but one who will actually be able to take away your sin and cleanse you forever."

All of it was God working so his people wouldn't miss Jesus. The reason Israelites needed a priest was to show them there had to be some sort of mediator between God and humans—which, of course, was Jesus. Also, once a year the High Priest would enter the place where he gave a sacrifice and would sprinkle blood on the mercy seat seven times. Under the mercy seat was the Ark of the Covenant where the Ten Commandments were hidden. It was God's way of pointing to the fact that because of his mercy, Jesus' blood was going to cover those righteous requirements for us. He is the ultimate fulfillment of the Old Testament.

That fact is actually what led early Romans to consider the first Christians atheists. They'd ask, "Where is your temple?" to which the Christians would reply that they didn't have a building, and Jesus was their temple. So then they'd ask, "Well, who is your priest?" To which they'd reply that they didn't have a priest on earth, because Jesus was their ultimate priest in heaven. Finally they'd ask, "Who is your sacrifice?" to which the early Christians would respond that they no longer offered sacrifices because Jesus' sacrifice was once for all.[3]

That is what Jesus meant when he said, "I have not come to abolish [the Law or the Prophets] but to fulfill them." That truth changes someone from dead, man-made religion to a vibrant relationship with Jesus and his body.

## THE MEANING BEHIND

Back in my dorm room, I was trying to put all these thoughts down for the students I was talking with who wanted nothing to do with religion. I knew we needed a common starting point for any conversation about Jesus to get off the ground and decided on this: "So know I hate religion. In fact, I literally resent it. Because when Jesus cried, 'It is finished,' I believe he meant it."

While the poem did resonate with my peers, I need to clarify that when I say I "hate" religion, I am not saying I hate the church.

I'm not saying I hate commandments, traditions, or laws.

I'm not saying I hate organizations or institutions.

But what I am saying is that I hate any system that upholds moral effort or good behavior as the way in which we can have a proper relationship with God. My main problem with religion, how I defined it, is if that is possible—the fact we can just be "good enough" for God—then that is spitting in the face of Jesus. That's mocking him, saying his sacrifice isn't good enough and wasn't necessary.

One of my favorite hobbies is reading. I love reading. Alyssa jokes with me that my "love language" is books. I think it's true. I like books so much that when I started getting more than I had room for, my then-roommate and I got bunk beds to free up more space for books. I don't know what's more lame, though—that I just admitted my favorite hobby is reading, or that I just admitted I was twenty-three and still slept in a bunk bed.

Anyway, I started to notice this vein in a lot of strong theologian-type people, people who are seen as giants of the church. People like John Owen, Tim Keller, Oswald Chambers, and A. W. Tozer.

Even the famous German theologian Dietrich Bonhoeffer wanted to get to a place of "religionless Christianity." In 1944, while he was in prison for trying to sabotage the Nazis, he wrote, "We are moving towards a completely religionless age; people as they are now simply cannot be religious anymore. Even those who honestly describe themselves as 'religious' do not in the least act up to it, and so they presumably mean something quite different by 'religious.'"[4]

Bonhoeffer knew that the term *religious* had become stale, so he fought for something entirely new. He actually found it helpful to juxtapose religion and Jesus.

Now, I love the word *religion*, in its true sense, and it's helpful in some cases, but I've also noticed it's the easiest way to expose someone who trusts in their own works, which is a major problem today. In a postmodern world where all religious activity is seen as what we do for God, we need to proclaim Christianity is about what God has done for us. This would take people's focus off of their behavior and put it on Jesus.

When you distinguish Jesus the God-man from the religion that developed around him, people investigate the person of Jesus rather than the rules of Christianity. And the truth is, when someone is pursuing, investigating, and attempting to understand the Son of God, he or she is pursuing truth personified, and that person will find him.

The minute I started to frame the discussions in this way, there was an interesting change. A lot of people didn't want to talk about religion, but seemed fine talking about Jesus. When we studied Jesus, we could actually look stuff up.

He said what?

He did what?

And the facts often shocked my friends. The Jesus of the Scriptures is so much more radical and subversive than we realize. That's why I wrote the poem. I wanted to write a poem that a few hundred college students would hear and remember. One they'd take to class with them the next day. One that would make us actually have to talk about Jesus. When religious discussions are broad and consider the ideas of theologians rather than the facts about Jesus, they generate apathetic views of Jesus. Changing the focus of the conversation from religion to Jesus actually invites people to face him and the grace he provides. It lets his grace so confront them that they have to address it.

The response that proved this is when I'd ask my friends about Jesus and they'd say, "He's a nice guy." Or, "He had good moral principles, but he's not God."

Sadly, that's one of the most unintelligent things a person can say. If Jesus claimed to be God, claimed to forgive sins, and claimed to heal the sick, then he either did those things, or he was a despicable liar. Either he is who he says he is—God—or he has deceived billions and billions for the last two thousand years. That wouldn't make him a good moral teacher; it would make him the most damnable person on earth. Either he's God, or he deserves to be cast into human history as one of the worst. And that's why, in my conversations with others, I take the focus off what we do for God and put it on what he has done for us so we have to actually deal with him.

We can talk theory until we are blue in the face. We can talk about what the word *God* even means. But you start investigating and pushing into this guy from Nazareth who lived two thousand years ago, and you *will* get somewhere. You *will* have to face up to who he is, what he has done, and what you will do about it.

Be careful when you pursue truth, because you just might find him.

1. Jeff describes the brokenness he witnessed while he was an RA, a brokenness that remained largely hidden. What drives us to keep our brokenness hidden from others, and what does that cost us?

2. Jeff writes, "My generation is the most fatherless and insecure generation that's ever lived, and we are willing to sacrifice everything if we can just be told we are loved." Do you agree with this assessment? Why or why not?

3. Why do you think Christianity's essence has devolved to "hates gays, can't drink beer, and no tattoos" in the minds of so many? Is this a result of the institutional church, individual Christians, or something else?

4. How has the Christian faith been more about good advice rather than good news in your experience?

5. If relationship with Jesus is the new law, how does that influence your understanding of rules or expectations within Christian faith communities? Does it shift your understanding about an external code? If so, how?

6. Jeff claims that he hates any system that promotes moral behavior as the only way to have a proper relationship with God. Do you agree? Why or why not?

7. How is the Jesus portrayed in the Gospels different from the Jesus promoted by religion?

8. If God doesn't want rule-followers, what does he expect from us as believers in Jesus?

# CHAPTER 3

# FUNDIES, FAKES, AND OTHER SO-CALLED CHRISTIANS

I was watching TV the other day when I came across really angry people on the news talking about God's judgment and wrath. They held up signs that read, "God Hates Fags." Confused and angry, I turned the channel. On the next channel was one of those music award shows. After I watched a few acceptance speeches, I noticed each artist was thanking God for the award. I thought, *Hmm, never knew any of them to be the religious type.*

To be honest, I didn't know which one made me angrier: that weird person on the street corner who tells everyone they're going to hell—with signs so outdated you'd think they used those same ones when they picketed Jesus' funeral—or the hip-hop artist who thanks Jesus for winning a Grammy for his song about naked women, Grey Goose, and stacks of money. I'm convinced that every time God hears one of those speeches he gets sick.

Sadly, those are two of the most common representations of Jesus that drive many people away. Either people can't possibly bear to be in the same family as the wacko, or they think Jesus is irrelevant and doesn't actually change anyone's life—like the rapper giving the acceptance speech. Both are wrong, though.

All the reasons my peers oppose Jesus are the same reasons Jesus opposed both the hyperfundamentalist and the fake. We discussed in chapter 1 how he opposed the self-righteous Pharisees, but think about how his preaching repels people who want to wear the cross and not live it. In the book of Mark, Jesus is feeding four thousand people with only a few loaves of bread and some fish. You can imagine the crowd's awe and enjoyment. Jesus was becoming a rock star. You better believe he would have had TMZ following him at this point.

From there he goes and heals a man at Bethsaida. Everyone sees Jesus' power and wants more. So what does he do?

Does he revel in the attention?
Leverage his fame as an evangelistic tool?
Ask people to bow their heads and close their eyes
   and raise their hands for him?

He actually does the opposite. He says, "If anyone would come after me, let him deny himself and take up his cross and follow me. For whoever would save his life will lose it, but whoever loses his life for my sake and the gospel's will save it."[1]

If Jesus wanted to grow a church, didn't he know telling people they need to daily pick up an instrument of torture, death, and shame wasn't the way to do it? Jesus opposed the pharisaical legalism of his time, but he also opposed the watered-down, flimsy, cultural religion. He was essentially saying, "I know my miracles are awesome. I know I have immense power. But don't follow me for the wrong reason. The cost is high. The road to follow me is tough, it's painful, it hurts, and you might even face death, but I promise there is joy on the other side. Do you want in?"

To some degree we all tend to misrepresent Jesus. Are you sometimes cold, aloof, and prideful? Are you inclined to see Jesus as your puppet giving you freedom to do whatever you'd like "in his name"? Or maybe for you church is just a hobby or obligation, no different from getting a haircut. Or maybe you love ideas about Jesus rather than Jesus himself.

I only recently realized how much I fell into one of the distortions. In the depths of my heart, if I'm brutally honest, I still wickedly think I am better than other people. You know how I know? When something bad happens to someone I don't like, I think, *Yes! He finally got what he deserved.* I forget that if I got what I deserve, I'd be in hell. Thank you, Jesus, for grace.

Sometimes I cling to religious rules and prideful self-righteousness rather than a humble living faith. We continually need to ask ourselves, do we really look like Jesus? Do we smell like him? Are we so close to his heart that people sense him when they are around us? My prayer is that I'm always seen as a poor, feeble dude who has found life, rather than as an arrogant, prideful guy who has all the answers.

## THE FUNDIES

Technically, the term *fundamentalism* means "adhering to or living by basic truths." By that definition most of us are fundamentalists. But the term in our modern American culture has taken on a more negative connotation that misrepresents Christians. For the sake of clarity, whenever I say *fundamentalist* in this section, I'm talking about that common negative caricature that is so prevalent today.

So who's a fundamentalist by our culture's standards? Everyone knows one when they see one. The typical caricature is the person who wears suits, plays a pipe organ, and reads the Left Behind series in some cabin in the woods. He's the guy on *Larry King* who makes me cringe when he's the "Christian" voice on the show. He sounds mean, bigoted, hateful, and sometimes stupid.

A fundamentalist tends to add rules to the Bible. Even though there are few to no credible passages—properly interpreted—in Scripture that call things such as alcohol and tattoos utterly sinful, some fundamentalists insist they are. They twist the verses until it seems clear our standing with God is based solely on whether or not we have ink on our skin or drink fermented grapes. Caring for the poor and serving the downtrodden? Who cares as long as you don't swear.

Man, if only they could have told Jesus that before he performed his first miracle of turning water into wine.[2]

Obviously there are Christians who truly love Jesus and who also hold strong convictions about tattoos and drinking, including some of my friends, my family, and my pastors. In no way am I poking fun at people who hold those convictions. I am referring to those who seem to hold their personal convictions higher than actual life-and-death salvation issues. The essence of a fundamentalist, in the negative sense of the word, is self-centered, basing personal righteousness solely on personal behavior. What they do defines who they are. They are slaves to their self-imposed morality and in turn become joyless and hypocritical.

It's passages such as the one found in the book of Matthew that make me wonder if Jesus was speaking with today's culture in mind. In it Jesus condemns the fundamentalist Jews of his day by saying to them, "Woe to you, scribes and Pharisees, hypocrites! For you tithe mint and dill and cumin, and have neglected the weightier matters of the law: justice and mercy and faithfulness."[3]

I find it quite humorous to think they actually thought

they earned God's favor by giving over little pinches from their spice racks.

But then, don't we do the same? Maybe more of us are like the stereotypical fundamentalist than we realize. What do we as American Christians offer that different cultures would probably laugh at?

We offer God good Christian behavior, but we
neglect weightier matters like justice and mercy.
We are so focused on legislating how the gay
community can live that we don't show them grace,
kindness, and respect.
We talk a lot about tithing, but the single mom next
door can't pay her rent.
We make sure to have our quiet times every
morning, but we couldn't care less about actually
conversing with Jesus.
We have never said the *f* word out loud, but we have
never prayed for our local homeless community
either.

All of that is fundamentalism. And the truth is, it's a terrible version of Christianity. There's no joy for the person practicing it, and it draws no one to Jesus.

It reminds me of a trick I used to do in high school. Don't worry, I wear it now, but in high school I hated to wear my seat belt. I was getting so many seat belt tickets that whenever

I saw a cop on the road, I'd quickly pull the seat belt across my chest, without ever actually clicking it in, and hold it by my right hip until the cop passed. Then it hit me one day: I was "buckling" simply not to get caught, when I should have been doing it to protect my life. Not to mention I was exerting just as much energy—if not more, since I had to hold it there—as I would have if I had properly worn my seat belt.

I sacrificed real safety for the appearance of safety—and it was more work! That is the essence of fundamentalism— living by the rules to stay out of trouble rather than seeing the rules as tools to bring us into intimacy and joy. We exchange relationship with God for a bunch of church games. We give an appearance of something that doesn't actually save, and even takes more work. Why would we do that? Apart from Jesus the whole Christian culture is bizarre. Without Jesus it's just a bunch of weird rituals, tiny cups, and stale crackers.

This distortion of Christianity doesn't work because it's neither what God is after, nor what God is like. All through the Gospels, we see a God of celebration, a God who throws parties.[4] Sometimes it's even commanded. Now, command- ing a party might sound legalistic, but, hey, if we are going to be legalistic about something, why not be legalistic about having some fun? After all, the rest of eternity is going to be a wedding feast where we enjoy one another and celebrate for- ever. Whenever I walk by the street preachers, I laugh under my breath, picturing just how uncomfortable they are going to be in heaven when everyone else is partying it up.

I once heard Matt Chandler, a prominent pastor in Dallas, compare religion to a bad marriage. He said, imagine you and your significant other are thinking about getting married, and so you seek a married couple for advice on how to do it right. What if when you approach them about how their marriage is doing, the husband says, "Well, it really sucks. Her cooking is terrible. I haven't loved her in years, but divorce isn't an option, so we are still together." Do you think Alyssa and I would think, *Aww, that sounds great. I can't wait to have a marriage like that!* Of course not.

So it is with God. There is no glory brought to God's name when people are doing something because it's an obligation, with no real enjoyment of their Creator. This is why the people on the street corner aren't speaking for God. Heaven isn't a place for people who are scared of hell; it's for people who love Jesus. The reason heaven is heavenly—full of joy, life, and bliss—is because we'll be with Jesus.

I remember reading the Bible again in college and absolutely loving the apostle Paul. He pulled no punches, spoke sharply, and usually had quite the sense of humor. The one passage that blew all the others out of the water is in the book of Galatians. Paul wrote this letter to the believers in Galatia who had begun to say Jesus' sacrifice wasn't enough to save and that believers had to add to it to make it effective. There was a group during Paul's time called the Judaizers who claimed you had to trust in Jesus for salvation and hold to Jewish laws such as circumcision to have a perfect relationship with God.

Basically, you had to become a Jew before you could convert to Christianity. As if the ones who just trusted in Jesus by faith were rookies or something.

Paul says the Galatians had missed the point. They had fallen away from the purity of the gospel. They had forgotten it's not Jesus plus their good behavior, but Jesus alone. Even in Bible times, Christians were quick to abandon the pure gospel. We so deeply want to contribute to our own salvation that we become intoxicated by the rules. Neither Jesus nor Paul allows that though. Jesus knew our tendency to emphasize external behavior when the gospel is a matter of transformation and faith in the heart.

I think the more focused Christians are on external behavior, the greater the possibility they are trying to make up for what they lack in their hearts. When we have no real transforming power of Jesus in our hearts, we hold up a list of external behaviors so someone can look at us and identify us as Christians. We humans prefer the tangible to the intangible any day. We prefer the flesh to the Spirit, the law to the heart.

The apostle Paul answers the Galatians by fighting verse after verse to show that we receive the Spirit of Jesus by faith as a gift, so why would we now think we could earn or work to keep it? It gets really good toward the end when Paul no longer holds back and shows his frustration: "But if I, brothers, still preach circumcision, why am I still being persecuted? In that case the offense of the cross has been removed. I wish those who unsettle you would emasculate themselves!"[5]

Did you catch that? Paul wished they would "emasculate" themselves. A quick Google search will tell you exactly what *emasculate* means. It means to take away one's manhood. *Ouch.* If the apostle Paul were around today, I wouldn't be surprised if he got kicked out of a few churches for a potty mouth like that.

I know circumcision is a weird spiritual issue for us today, but we aren't that different from the first-century Christians. Today some churches uphold baptism as their thing, some churches uphold how you dress, some churches uphold whether you are a Calvinist or an Arminian, but Paul says it's by grace alone, through faith alone, in Jesus alone. That's it.

Water doesn't save us.
Circumcision doesn't save us.
Calvin doesn't save us.
Jesus saves us.

## THE FAKES

Fakes are also pretty easy to spot. Most of them raised their hands in a Christian youth camp. If they were really solid, they raised their hands each night of the camp, getting saved all five nights of the week. They probably wear crosses around their necks, own a few Bibles, and check the Christian box under religious views on Facebook. Once they get into their twenties, fakes usually like to refer to themselves as *spiritual* not religious. While being a Christian involves being spiritual, most of the time the fakes use this description to forfeit any real accountability.

At the university I went to my first year, freshmen were encouraged to attend Bible studies. Because everyone on my hall went, I felt obligated to conform so I wouldn't be looked at as "that guy."

Prayed a prayer? *Check.*

Regularly attended Bible studies? *Check.*

Memorized John 3:16? *Check.*

Had a necklace or bracelet with a cross or fish? *Check.*

Actually loved, pursued, and enjoyed Jesus more

than anything? *Well, not so much.*

One particular night at Bible study stands out in my mind. It probably hadn't even been fifteen minutes after it finished, but I was already down by the beach smoking weed with some friends. My conscience began to accuse me of being a fake and a hypocrite, but I did my best to suppress it. I quickly realized I wasn't the only one. Going to a very conservative Christian college my freshman year, I was highly aware of the fakes. Takes one to know one, right? Most of us on the baseball team would pray after every practice only to be wrapped around a toilet throwing up just a few hours later. There were plenty of times we would sit around smoking weed on a Sunday, discussing whether or not we were going to go to the school's chapel the next the morning. And here's the thing: *we legitimately thought we were Christians.* When you are a hypocrite, you don't really like to stop and think about it, ya know?

Being in a college environment for the last four years of my life, I know hypocrisy drives people away from the church almost more than anything. The author Brennan Manning famously said, "The greatest single cause of atheism in the world today is Christians, who acknowledge Jesus with their mouths and walk out the door and deny him by their lifestyle."[6] In America anyone can say they're a Christian, and it means nothing. Unlike living in the Middle East as a Christian, no one gets stoned or beheaded here because they say they love Jesus. Sometimes I wonder what real persecution of Christians would reveal in America. Persecution, like fire, burns up the weak elements (wood and hay) but actually purifies the strong ones (silver and gold).

It still shocks me that when you approach fakes and ask pointed questions, they immediately get defensive and tell you about some past decision rather than what's going on in the present. Later in college when I was actually following Jesus, I had a friend on the baseball team who had numerous religious tattoos and wore a cross around his neck. When the team talked about deep spiritual things on the bus rides, he would be the first to give his opinion. But he was also the most explicit about his party life. He was the first to talk about how many girls he had slept with that weekend and how "crazy drunk" he got the night before.

I remember approaching him and simply asking in all gentleness, "Hey, man, just wondering how you see Jesus lining up with your lifestyle? Do you really think they're compatible?"

Instantly he went on about how he had gone to church his whole life and raised his hand to get "saved" when he was a kid.

We don't justify current bad behavior by citing past good behavior in other areas of our lives. No one does that with marriage. When a husband is cheating on his wife and is confronted, I'm guessing he doesn't say, "We got married ten years ago, so I can do whatever I want now. I gave my vows, right? That's proof that I'm a good husband."

So why do we do that with Jesus?

What would it look like if we treated our spouses or friends the way we treat God? What if we gave them 10 percent of all our money, talked to them a lot on Sundays, told everyone we were dating or married to them, but in exchange, asked if we could do whatever we wanted on all the other days? How would that work for us? If we did a few good things for them during the week, would we be free to then sleep with whomever we want, not talk to them, and lie to others about it all? Of course not. Yet that's what we do with God, and somehow we think he's down with that.

Some people think, *I got saved when I was ten, so Jesus is my homeboy, right?* Well, yes, but probably not in the way they mean it. He isn't okay with your sin. In fact, he hates it when you sin. From the moment we take a breath, we are cosmic rebels who commit holy treason against the Creator of the universe every second of every day. We give our allegiance to sex, alcohol, sports teams, and religion—but not Jesus. Shouldn't it make us tremble that every second of every day our lives are spitting in God's face, telling him we'd rather have his stuff than him? But he still keeps loving and pursuing us.

## THE REVERSE LEGALISTS

Self-righteousness is exactly that—thinking that your righteousness (your standing before God and others) relies only on yourself. You think you can earn it. You think it's about what you do or don't do. Because of this you are driven to act only in ways that continue to prop up how awesome you think you are. It produces a very prideful I-have-all-the-answers-and-you-are-all-idiots type of arrogance.

According to this definition, there might be some "religious" people in your midst who don't dress the part. Some of the most self-righteous people I have ever met have been twenty-year-old hipsters. Some of the most self-righteous people today are in the young generation. Arrogance seeps out of college campuses more than anywhere else.

I was sitting in an undergrad philosophy classroom when the discussion seemed to turn on me in a second. We were all giving our points of view and dialoguing about the issue at hand. As a Christian I offered my thoughts from a Christian worldview. Immediately I felt the distaste in the room as if I had just said something horribly wrong. Someone said, "You can't *possibly* think your way is the only way? How arrogant of you."

But I always wonder why we Christians are the ones who get slapped with the too-narrow-and-exclusive card when everyone's point of view is the same. Think about it: Every worldview is exclusive to itself. Even by that classmate saying I was arrogant for thinking my way was right, she was doing the same thing—saying I was wrong, and she was right. How arrogant of her—not really, but according to her own logic, yes.

I remember shooting back with a question, "How am I prideful for placing myself under an outside authority that has a track record of two thousand years with millions, if not billions, of people doing the same, when you seem to do whatever you want in life as an authority unto yourself simply because you are your own god? How does that make me more prideful? How am I the arrogant one?"

Another time someone asked me, "Why would I become a Christian? They're all just hypocrites!" To which I responded, "Yes, we are. Everyone is. Unless—surely you are not saying— that everyone is a hypocrite *except you*, right?"

In the Christian world, this self-righteous attitude is just as prevalent. It's in me, too, and I pray to God daily that he would eradicate the spirit within me that thinks I'm an authority unto myself. Because again, of course, we can think fundamentalists only wear suits and play boring Christian music, or we can address fundamentalism for what it is— an issue of the heart. Remember, fundamentalism is adding rules to the Bible, or elevating things beyond how Scripture elevates them.

There is a weird subsection of young Christians today who are almost reverse fundamentalists, but they are *still* fundamentalists. They look at the older generation who say in good conscience Christians shouldn't drink beer, and they respond, "We are definitely drinking beer." Or they see those Christians who say you have to dress up for church service, and they say, "We are only going to wear skinny jeans and V-neck T-shirts in church."

They are better defined by what they are against than by what they are for. They are doing the exact same thing as what they are defining themselves against. They are elevating behavior, clothing, and other secondary issues as requirements to gain access into the kingdom. It's a sickness in all of us to put our righteousness in absolutely *anything* except Jesus, and if we think we aren't doing that, it usually means it's even worse.

The fundamentalists of our parents' generation are still around, but they are not nearly as prevalent today. Fundamentalists don't always wear suits. Sometimes they wear skinny jeans. Sometimes they say you have to be able to drink beer to be a real Christian. Sometimes they only allow dirty grunge rock in their church service and make flannels mandatory to play in the worship band. Here's a quick note though: if you care more about flaunting your Christian freedom than promoting Christian unity, you're probably not free. You are actually a slave to your so-called freedom.

True freedom is being able to give up all your rights for another out of love. Just ask Jesus. He willingly came to earth. Willingly lived life for thirty-three years. Willingly let himself be beaten, scourged, and crucified. All for others. All for us.

## WE'RE ALL INVITED TO THE PARTY

Jesus illustrates the Father's love for all of us in the story of the prodigal son.[7] One son works hard to serve his father while another son asks for his inheritance and says, "Peace out," spending the money on parties and traveling till he's poor and literally eating with the pigs.

You may have heard the church version of this story, which focuses on the younger son living his Jersey Shore lifestyle, fist-pumping his way to debauchery, when he realizes it isn't working. Ashamed and broke, he reasons that his father would never love him as a son but that he could at least get a job as a servant, since even servants live better than he was. So he comes home ready to beg for a job, but instead of shunning him, the father runs to him, embraces him, and kisses him. He completely disregards the son's prepared apology speech and instead throws a party that would rival any on MTV's *Sweet 16* to celebrate his return home. He wanted to be an employee, but the father says, "No, you're a son." It's a beautiful picture of grace, redemption, and our heavenly Father's pursuit of us.

But that's only half of the story. Here's where it gets interesting: The parable of the prodigal son was told to the religious people, not the rebellious. So why do we put all the focus on the rebellious son? What about the other son?

Before telling this story, the writer Luke records that the Pharisees were grumbling and complaining because Jesus "receives sinners and eats with them."[8] Religious folks haven't changed a lot since then, huh? One of the best barometers of a true Christian's heart is to see what kind of people he attracts and what kind of people he repels. If Jesus is in you, you should attract the marginalized and beaten-down members in society, just as he did. And there will be some people who aren't happy with it.

Jesus told the parable to the Pharisees as a response to their grumbling and complaining. This is important because the point of the parable isn't just the redemption of the younger son. It's also about the older son's reaction to the redemption of the younger son. We think Jesus told the story for the younger brother, but that first verse is an indicator that the story was told specifically for the more religious older brother.

The Bible says, "Now his older son was in the field, and as he came and drew near to the house, he heard music and dancing."[9] The older brother heard a celebration. I wonder what he thought was going on. Up to this point, I'm sure he didn't even know his brother had returned. Maybe he thought his old man was having a midlife crisis, called a DJ, and hung up some streamers.

When he finds out the party is for his wayward brother now returned home, the Bible says, "He was angry and refused to go in."[10] *That's not fair,* he thinks. *I've worked hard for Dad. I've been good for Dad. My brother? A loser who wasted our family fortune. Why does he get a party and I get nothing?*

In anger he confronts his father: "Look, these many years I have served you, and I never disobeyed your command, yet you never gave me a young goat, that I might celebrate with my friends. But when this son of yours came, who has devoured your property with prostitutes, you killed the fattened calf for him!"[11]

Some of us are like the older brother. We've been good, so we think the Father owes us good gifts. And we think that others are so bad that they deserve nothing from the Father.

Others of us are like the younger brother. We're ashamed of our pasts and think we don't deserve any good gifts from our Father. But the reality is that the Father gives his good gifts freely to whomever he chooses as a radical act of love and grace.

To the wayward children he says, "Bring the fattened calf and kill it, and let us eat and celebrate. For this my son was dead, and is alive again; he was lost, and is found."[12]

To those of us who think we're Ned Flanders from *The Simpsons,* God looks past our pride and graciously invites us to the party, saying, "You are always with me, and all that is mine is yours. It was fitting to celebrate and be glad, for this your brother was dead, and is alive; he was lost, and is found."[13]

What I love about the story is that not once does the father look at the older son and say, "Fine; be that way. Your younger brother and I are going to party!"

No, it says he goes out and talks with the older brother. He entreats him. No one is more religious than the Christian who gives grace to everyone except the religious older-brother types. God gives grace to the younger and the older. No one is past redemption. No one is past grace. All God wants is for both the religious and the rebellious to come into the party. We can wallow in self-righteousness, or we can enjoy all that is our Father's.

The reality is that the father owed neither son anything, and both sons showed ungratefulness in different ways.

The younger son was foolish. The older son was
   prideful.
The younger son was physically lost. The older son
   was spiritually lost.
The younger son didn't want the father's love. The
   older son thought he could earn the father's love.

We children of God have been acting the same since the beginning of time toward our Father God. Yet he invites us to enjoy him and all that is his. Like both the older and younger brothers, we must learn that the joy of our lives is not in what we get from the Father but how we get to be with him as his children. He's throwing a party, and we are all invited.

The reality is that it's harder for religious people to come to Christ than anyone else because they think they are already good to go. In the parable of the prodigal son, we know that the younger brother is happy to receive the grace of the father. But Jesus never tells us if the older brother does. There's no conclusion. The father entreats him, but there is no indication as to how the older brother responds to his dad's invitation.

Jesus leaves the story open-ended as an invitation to us "older brothers." He's essentially asking, will you join the party?

No matter how we come to Jesus—whether we are coming to him for the first time or finding our way back to him after faking it, or even if we have tried to be righteous by adding our own rules to the Bible—we are all in need of his grace and truth. We won't find Jesus in the rapper on TV or in the person yelling at us from the street corner or in the baseball player attending a Bible study one minute and smoking weed the next. Sometimes we misinterpret truth, while other times we misinterpret grace.

But the God of the Bible is a loving Father who is full of both grace *and* truth.

1. Jeff would admit that he sometimes clings to religious rules or dead orthodoxy rather than living faith. What about you?

2. Why do you think some rules—such as prohibitions against alcohol, swearing, and tattoos—are given more weight in religious circles than caring for the poor and downtrodden?

3. Has the general Christian response to the gay community shown mercy, justice, and faithfulness? Why or why not?

4. Jeff states, "Heaven isn't a place for people who are scared of hell; it's for people who love Jesus." What's your understanding of heaven?

5. "When we have no real transforming power of Jesus in our hearts, we still want to act as we always have, so we hold up a list of external behaviors so others can look at us and still see we're Christians." Has this been your experience? Explain.

6. If the kind of people you attract and repel reveals the authenticity of your faith, how are you doing?

7. In the parable of the two sons, the father wants both to enjoy the party. Are you more likely to resist or take part? Why?

# CHAPTER 4

# RELIGION
## MAKES ENEMIES /
# JESUS MAKES FRIENDS

What started as a normal night bowling with friends turned out to be something quite different. When my buddies and I showed up at the local alley and began to bowl, we noticed a group of guys. We recognized them as the cool kids at the other local high school that had just opened up. These kids had transferred after going to high school with us for the first two years, but for some reason, the minute they changed schools and became the new crosstown rivals, we no longer spoke.

The bowling alley was full of tension. The football season had just ended, during which some things had happened that went far beyond friendly competition. They didn't like us. We didn't like them. We gave each other dirty looks, but it seemed we had all chosen to mind our own business.

Until we left. That's when I got a text from one of the girls with them. They were telling her to relay a few things to us about how they felt. Being typical guys hyped up on high school testosterone, we weren't going to take it. We told them to meet us at the local park in a few hours. We'd settle it fair and square. They agreed.

Because we knew a lot of people had been waiting to have this showdown between schools, we decided to call all the guys we knew would want in. Little did we know the group from the other high school was doing the same. We showed up at the park, and between all of us there had to have been at least 150 guys. The yelling started, we continued to get closer, and it was about to get ugly. Which is when we heard sirens. Chaos immediately broke out. Everyone running, hopping fences, and driving away as quickly as possible.

It was the biggest adrenaline spike I had ever experienced. At first I was mad it was all for nothing. But I have to believe those sirens were a gift from God. The next day we heard that a guy from one of the local gangs had shown up with a gun.

If the cops hadn't show up at that moment, it would not have gone well, and who knows what would have happened if weapons had come out. Why were we even there? Why was I about to fight with guys who had been my friends just a few years before? Why had I put myself in that position?

We are trained to make enemies. We are trained to assert ourselves above and against one another. We look for anything to pit ourselves against another. From birth it's always "us versus them." As a senior in high school, I was supposed to dislike the freshmen. As a baseball player, I was supposed to hit the opposing batter with my fastball if he did anything disrespectful.

Black vs. whites.

Conservatives vs. liberals.

Rich vs. poor.

Republican vs. Democrat.

Americans vs. whoever we're at war with.

Yankees vs. Red Sox. (If you've ever been to a game between these two, you can hardly call their rivalry trivial. New York and Boston have both had their fair share of crime after league games.[1])

It starts so early that we don't even notice. We love to pit ourselves against others. It gives us moral authority. It gives us moral affirmation.

Let's be honest: sometimes Christians are the worst. Our church is better than the one down the street. The way we do worship is better than worship in the church we grew up in.

Calvinists vs. Arminians.

Complementarians vs. egalitarians.

Charismatics vs. cessationists.

Catholics vs. Protestants.

As if the world dying outside really cares.

Now, I'm not saying some of these clarifications and differences aren't necessary. In the book of John, Jesus prays we would be "one."[2] The only way to become one is to engage in healthy discussion on topics we disagree on. But we can't honestly think any non-Christian will want to come into the family of God if we are just as—if not more—divisive than the rest of the world. Sometimes *how* we dialogue in today's culture is just as important as *why* we dialogue.

## RELIGION'S HIT LIST

Religion, unfortunately, is notorious for making enemies. Women? Gays? Muslims? Let's make them our enemies. Yes, I know this doesn't represent everyone. Yes, I know religion doesn't do this all the time. But throughout history, it is clear that when it does happen, it can almost always be traced back to people who think their standing with God comes from their own righteousness. Even proclaimed nonreligious men such as Stalin and Hitler acted out of their moral superiority, their self-righteousness.[3] It's just the way it works. The minute you think you have gotten on God's good side by your own behavior, you are naturally prone to demonize those who haven't.

And don't think this is something that happened "back

then." All we have to do is turn on any TV news station to see who the Christian enemies are supposed to be. The biggest difference between religious people and gospel-loving people is that religious people see certain *people* as the enemies, when Jesus-followers see *sin* as the enemy.

Last time I checked, I was my own worst enemy. No one has caused me more grief, pain, or heartache than I have. The Bible rarely tells me to fight against someone who doesn't believe what I believe, but it frequently tells me to fight against my sin and the disease in me that's drawing me away from Jesus.[4]

Religious people see "them" as the problem; Jesus-followers see "us" as the problem. When Jesus told the first disciples to love their enemies,[5] he didn't add, "as long as they look like you, talk like you, and act like you." Loving an enemy means loving "them." It's sad that someone like Martin Luther King Jr. is seen as a radical for obeying basic Christian principles. There isn't one verse in the Scripture that tells me to fight for my political party. Or fight to get prayer in public school. In fact, the times in history when Christianity was most persecuted and least governmentally sanctioned, it flourished most.[6]

I remember the moment this first hit home for me. I was having lunch with my mom in a cheap hole-in-the-wall restaurant that always served amazing food. As we started to eat, I felt the tension. I was a Christian now, and my mom was openly gay. Wasn't I supposed to hate her? Wasn't I told "not to associate" with her?[7] Doesn't she know homosexuals will not inherit the kingdom of God?

Instead I made a decision to listen. She was my mom. I listened as she poured out her thoughts, emotions, and feelings that had been pent up for years. I heard how she had been burned by certain religious communities—brutal stories of so-called Christians offering grace and redemption to all those around her, as long as the sin was socially acceptable. The sad part is, I couldn't disagree. I'd seen the same thing.

How many times had I heard a worship leader who had probably looked at porn the night before tell the church that being gay was a sin? How many times did I hear an obese pastor who was a slave to food tell the church that homosexuals were going to hell? Or what about the small-group leader who has been divorced four times telling us how wrong being gay is? I always found it unusual that the Bible talks more about divorce than homosexuality, but we hardly like to talk about that in the church. Why is the spotlight always on them? Does anyone else think it's weird that people actually picket gay-based events, but you never see a bunch of gay people picketing KFC or Old Country Buffet?

For some reason the church had made homosexuality a varsity sin, and my mom had felt the weight of it. Religious people are very particular and selective on this issue. My favorite is when they quote the 1 Corinthians passage. Let's take a quick look: "Do not be deceived: neither the sexually immoral, nor idolaters, nor adulterers, nor men who practice homosexuality, nor thieves, nor the greedy, nor drunkards, nor revilers, nor swindlers will inherit the kingdom of God. And such were some of you. But you were washed, you were sanctified, you were justified in the name of the Lord Jesus Christ and by the Spirit of our God."[8]

I don't see homosexuality getting any prominence in this list, do you? In fact, the apostle Paul is attempting to broad stroke everyone, highlighting the fact that none of us are good enough. To those who want to pick and choose from this verse, let's look at the others:

Ever had a lustful thought? Looked at porn? *Guilty.*
Ever wanted something more than God? *Yep.*
Ever looked at or engaged with someone else besides
    your spouse? *Ouch.*
Ever stolen? *I have.*
Ever had an insatiable desire for more money? *Check.*
Ever been drunk? *Double check.*
Ever reviled? *I don't even know what that means, but
    I'm sure I'm guilty of this too.*

I don't know about you, but I'm not scoring too well on this list. But how does that verse end? The Corinthians were undoubtedly filthy themselves and were not representing Christ well. Some of them were probably still engaging in these behaviors, which is why Paul was writing them the

letter, but he still says, "But you were washed, you were sanctified, you were justified in the name of the Lord Jesus Christ
and by the Spirit of our God."

He reminds them of how they've been bought.
He reminds them that their sins aren't their identities.
He reminds them they are different now and can
    walk *away* from their sins.

That is a scandalous statement! Paul says to them, "You
*were* washed." The best part about that verse is it doesn't seem
like the Corinthians had much to do with the washing. It doesn't
say, "but you washed yourself and cleaned up." No, it says they
"were washed." An outside force did the washing. And that's the
message of grace. If you are a Christian and are going to talk
about 1 Corinthians 6:9–10, then you better include verse 11.

It's only when we understand that in Jesus we are cleansed,
washed, and renewed that we see our sin fall by the wayside. We
didn't pull ourselves up by our bootstraps. We are greedy, filthy,
idolatry-loving, glory-hungry thieves. And when we trust Jesus,
he washes us. He redeems us—all of us. And when we're sitting
across the table from someone whom we've been told to hate,
the least we can do is listen and love her as Jesus loves us.

Regarding homosexuality specifically, I can't begin to tell
you the internal wrestling I've had with this issue. I have a
personal stake in it, so for me, it's much more than an abstract
idea. It's part of one of the closest people to me.

The one who raised me.

The one who provided for me.

The one who sacrificed for me.

So if I can be honest, I've gone back and forth a ton on this issue. Is it okay? Is it wrong? Why or why not?

And this is something I want to get across. Everything in me wanted to be convinced it was okay. Everything in me looked for verses to see it sanctioned by God. But through years of wrestling, hours of Bible study, and tons of prayer, I didn't come to that conclusion. When I open the Scriptures, I see homosexuality getting no prominence among sins, but it is still a distortion of God's creative order nonetheless.

But here's the thing: my mom and I disagree on it, and we *still* love each other.

Did you catch that? *We still love each other.*

We have open, honest, and sometimes very difficult conversations about it. And neither of us walks away calling the other a bigot. Neither of us walks away furious or upset. Because that's what love is.

It stays.

It pursues.

It pushes in.

And my mom has taught that to me better than anyone else has. So I want to say this loud and clear: in order for our society to continue to flourish, it is imperative that we learn how to have healthy, honoring, and engaging discussions on this issue.

The reason I think it is so tough for us to engage on this topic is because both sides feel like their identities are being attacked. It's not just something they do, but something they think they are. A gay person usually says, "This is who I am, and I can't change." And so when their sexuality is addressed, it feels like a personal attack. The same holds true for the Christian. When Christians are attacked on this issue for being bigoted or hateful, they say being a Jesus follower is who they are. It's difficult to have discussions on this topic because when we engage it, we are addressing each other's perceived identity. But if we can suspend that for a second and hold truth as external, maybe we will get somewhere.

But can we stop calling each other names and resorting to living in our little tribes? I always laugh when someone calls me a bigot because the closest gay person to me doesn't think that, and she actually knows me and has a right to call me that if she wishes.

In America, we pride ourselves on being a pluralist society. But true pluralism is every rational worldview getting a voice in the marketplace. True pluralism is people living close to others who share different views. But in America, we call each other names, retreat to our own camps where everyone thinks and talks as we do, and that's not pluralism. That's tribalism—and you lose the real definition of love when you live in that kind of society.

## LIMPING ACROSS THE FINISH LINE

Avoiding sin isn't about us not getting in trouble; it is about us trusting that the Creator knows his creation best and has designed the world to work in a certain way. Everything outside of his creative order is a distortion, and when we follow that fractured path, we are implying we are our own gods and know better than he does. The issue isn't primarily homosexuality, idolatry, drunkenness, greed, or right or wrong. The issue is, are we going to trust that God knows best or that our thoughts, wills, and emotions know best?

I'm just going to come out and say it: People don't go to hell because they are gay. Ever. Never in a million years will God send someone to hell for being gay. People go to hell because they want to be the gods of their own lives. People go to hell because they want to be kings. They want to determine what is right or wrong.

The truth is we are all going to limp across the finish line to some degree. Of course there is victory in Jesus, and of course we are more than conquerors through Christ as the apostle Paul says; but even Paul had a thorn in the flesh.[9] Most of us have a spiritual Achilles' heel. We all will have spiritual bruises, cuts, and sores. Some will limp across the finish line still fighting their addiction to porn. Some will limp across the finish line with their addiction to food. And some will limp across the finish line with their attraction to the same sex.

The issue isn't whether someone is good or bad, but

whether he is repentant or unrepentant. Who is God of her life? Who's in control? What or who are they pursuing? Are they looking to him or trusting in self? Because I trust that if Jesus' grace has radically collided with a heart, I believe that person will begin to align themselves with Jesus' image, looking more like him every day.

But let's also realize that we do have hope and victory and are called to take sin very seriously, doing anything and everything to run from it and to Jesus. The writer of Hebrews makes it clear by saying we should "also lay aside every weight, and sin which clings so closely, and . . . run with endurance the race that is set before us, looking to Jesus, the founder and perfecter of our faith."[10]

Even he admits there are things that weigh us down. Our sin sticks to us almost the way lint sticks to something after you take it out of the dryer. But still . . . he says run with endurance, looking to Jesus. Don't take your eyes off him. He is the author of our faith and the finisher of it. Keep our eyes on him, and we will make it because it depends on him, not us. But let us never get prideful. Let us never think this race is reserved for the elite, or the "good," or the well qualified. It's reserved for the lowly, the rejected, the marginalized.

One of my favorite stories in the Bible is the story of the woman at the well (in the book of John in the New Testament).[11] She is the first person to whom Jesus reveals himself to be the messiah. Isn't that interesting? Jesus doesn't choose to share this information first with a politician or a king or anyone of seeming importance, but with a Samaritan woman.

Just to give some background, in New Testament times Samaritans were seen as half-breed Jews, products of an impure mixture between a Jew and a gentile. They were looked down upon by the Jews. On top of this she was a woman, which in that culture meant she was a second-class citizen. Even worse, Jesus highlights her promiscuity and how she had a string of intimate relationships with guys whom she would then marry and most likely divorce shortly after. In the middle of all this, Jesus reveals the truth about himself to her. She is the first to know Jesus is the messiah in the book of John! And Jesus doesn't condemn this woman either for her promiscuity, but rather graciously shows how he is the "living water" that can quench her insatiable thirst.

So Jesus, God himself, showed immense grace and gave great privilege to a half-breed, second-class, adulterous, and promiscuous woman. And he did that on purpose. God is always a fan of going to the marginalized so his saving power isn't credited to human wisdom but to his grace. Jesus completely shattered the social, gender, and economic paradigms. Such barriers didn't exist to him, and it was the same in the early church. New Testament Christians were most known by their love for their neighbors, but today we are most known for our segregation of the lowly.

The way I see it, this issue really comes down to idolatry,

which is the act of placing anything or anyone above Jesus as the ultimate source of worth, satisfaction, and identity. The problem with idolatry, though, is that whatever you idolize, you then demonize the opposite. So you can tell if people idolize politics by whether or not they demonize the opposite side of the aisle. Sure, a Republican can disagree and dialogue with a Democrat, but if a Republican thinks Democrats are the source of all evil, that's a sign of an idol, a worthless, fake god. If you idolize your self-righteousness, then you demonize those who are "evil" or "worldly" and not like you.

Want to know what you probably idolize? Ask what you demonize. But when you idolize Jesus, then you demonize demons—which makes a lot of sense to me. When Jesus and his righteousness are ultimate, then you actually see evil as the source of evil, rather than politics, money, or gender. Sure, you can disagree. Sure, you can have dialogue; but when something is your god, you'll go to great lengths to defend it.

While I don't agree with most of his viewpoints, Bill Maher said something that completely makes sense.

> New rule: If you're a Christian who supports killing your enemies and torture, you have to come up with a new name for yourself. . . .
>
> "Capping thine enemy" is not exactly something Jesus would do. . . .
>
> I'm not even judging you. I'm just saying logically, if

you ignore every single thing Jesus commanded you to do, you're not a Christian. You're just auditing.

You're not Christ's followers. You're just fans.[12]

So what do you say we start taking what Jesus said seriously and stop pretending like we actually care? The truth is, since Bill isn't a Christian, I sometimes think I can dismiss what he says. *He doesn't know what he's talking about. How dare he say that?* But the truth is, he's right. So if you are still investigating Jesus but have been turned off by many so-called Christians' treatment of certain people, know they might not be Christians, just auditors. And if we say we love Jesus, let's start acting like followers and stop acting like fans. The world is waiting, and they can tell the difference.

1. Why is it so hard to love "them"?
2. Jeff says he's intrigued that Christianity flourished the most when it was under persecution and not sanctioned by the government. Why do you think that is the case?
3. Have you ever tried washing yourself from your sin rather than letting Jesus do this work of grace?
4. Describe what most attracts you to the person of Jesus.
5. Jeff suggests that idolatry is "the act of placing anything or anyone above Jesus as the ultimate source of worth, satisfaction, and identity." Why do we place other things above Jesus in our lives? Where do you find your worth, satisfaction, and identity?
6. If you were truly to follow Jesus, what would be different in your life?

# CHAPTER 5

# WITH RELIGION, THERE ARE GOOD AND BAD PEOPLE / WITH JESUS, THERE ARE ONLY BAD PEOPLE IN NEED OF GRACE

Back when I played baseball in college, the team traveled on a lot of buses for our games and tournaments. Sometimes the trip would be a few hours; sometimes it would be a few days. As a collegiate athlete, you have no choice but to get used to bus life. My teammates and I would pack as many snacks as we could fit in our bags, make a few playlists on our iPods, and bring our homework. A lot of times, rather than doing homework, we would get into good conversations with each other.

I remember one conversation I had with a teammate about the basic teachings of Jesus. I gave him facts about why they were historically reliable, and he shot back a few reasons why they weren't. I loved it—wrestling, thinking, engaging. But then I hit a roadblock when I said, "Jesus paid for your sins, and you don't need to hold on to them anymore." My friend responded, "I know Jesus maybe did that for the murderers and child molesters, but I haven't killed anyone. I'm not that bad."

The funny thing was, that wasn't the last time I heard that particular response. I probably had a similar conversation hundreds of times while in college. Students just kept insisting they weren't "that bad." They think, *I haven't killed anyone, I pay my taxes, I am nice to people, and most of all, I'm better than most people around me. God must love me.*

The problem we have with Jesus isn't that he gives life and grace freely, but that we have to admit our need for it. It's hard to convince people Jesus is a great savior when they don't think they need saving.

## GRADING ON A CURVE

In college I majored in politics and government. My early hope was either to be a lawyer or teach social studies and government at my local high school. The soft sciences (sociol ogy, political science, etc.) came much easier to me than the hard sciences (anatomy, chemistry, etc.). I remember having to take a biology course, and while it was interesting, it was like a foreign language. This played out in my test scores too. But what was awesome about that class was the professor graded on a curve, which meant the professor took the highest score, made that the new 100 percent, and recalculated the other scores with that in mind.

For people like me, grading on a curve was great. I always knew I'd do poorly on the tests, so instead of studying really hard and praying I'd do well, I just prayed that no one would get a really good grade so it would all even out. My test scores weren't held to a solid standard; they were viewed in comparison to others.

Let's be honest: we think that's what God does. We like to think that God is a professor scowling through the bifocals resting on his nose and grading all our behavior on a curve. Statistically, when a professor grades on a curve, there are a few really high achievers, most of the class is in the middle, and then some fail even after the score readjustment—a classic bell curve. That is how a lot of us see humanity. Martin Luther King Jr. and Gandhi get As, then all of us are in the middle, and Hitler and Stalin still fail.

We point to the greats of society and say, "Well, only a select few can be them," and then we turn to the worst of history and say, "Well, I'm not as bad as them, so I must be going to heaven." But the truth is, God doesn't grade on a curve; he grades on a cross. Trying to be good enough to earn heaven is like trying to jump to Hawaii from the coast of California. Everyone looks like an idiot, some drown, some get three feet, some get ten feet, but no one even gets close to Hawaii.

If that's the way you think, I understand. That was me, too, for nineteen years of my life. For as long as I can remember, I was a good kid. My parents, my teachers, and my coaches all told me this. When I got to high school, I was the kid who didn't do the "bad" things. I mean, who cares if I got kicked out of school in middle school, started watching porn daily, and had outbursts of anger? I had excuses for all of those. It's because my dad didn't teach me how to be a man. It's because everyone does it, right? I was still basically a good person. I didn't kill anyone. I respected adults.

My identity, my worth, and my purpose in life were wrapped up in my behavior and earning others' approval. Because of this I sacrificed my life trying to make others think I was a good person. Who cares if I actually was? I just wanted others to think I was. All my energy was devoted to keeping people's perceptions of me in good standing. I wonder how many others behave this way. As long as others think we are good, we really don't care what our lives actually look like. Outside reputation is more valuable than personal transformation.

Then in high school I played on a baseball team whose coach was a solid Christian. I remember him giving a talk at one practice and he asked a question that just haunted me. He was talking about how we humans concentrate so much on the outside, but how God cares more about what's going on inside. He then asked me, "Jeff, if I hooked up a projector to your brain, and we watched every thought you'd had in the last hour, what would we see? What about last month? Your whole life?"

In that moment I knew I was caught. If anyone saw my thoughts, then I'd probably never show my face ever again. God actually sees that. Every thought. And while seeing it, he says, "I'm going to go rescue Jeff," with a smile on his face. That blew my mind. I realized that fighting to prove I was good enough was actually the one thing keeping me out of heaven. A grace economy is backward to most of us—those who think they qualify, don't; and those who admit they don't qualify, do. There's no bell curve involved.

## THE DEADLY COMPARISON GAME

Recently I was in Uganda visiting an orphanage in a rural part of the country. It was beautiful and peaceful. One of the smaller differences I noticed between how they live and how kids in America live is that they only had one mirror on the entire premises, and most of the kids rarely wandered to where it was. Because of this, kids would use other means to see their reflections. They'd rely on friends telling them, they'd look in water, or they'd simply go without seeing themselves for long periods of time. If one of the kids looked at his reflection in a pile of mud, would that give him an accurate portrayal of himself? Of course not. If mud was mixed with enough rain, it might give *some* picture, but mud would extremely distort his reflection.

Isn't this what we do when we compare ourselves to others? Always finding the least moral person we know and comparing ourselves to that person to make us feel better is like looking at our reflections in a pool of mud. It won't accurately show us who we are, so why do we trust it? If we want to know what we really look like, we have to look in pure, clean, smooth water. That would give us a clear picture. And that is what Jesus does.

Jesus is that pure, undefiled water in which we instantly see our inadequacies. You might say, "Well, I've never cheated on my significant other!" According to Jesus, you probably have. "You have heard that it was said, 'You shall not commit adultery.' But I say to you that everyone who looks at a woman with lustful intent has already committed adultery with her in his heart."[1] Ouch. It seems Jesus didn't come to lower the standard; he actually came to raise it. He took the issue from external to internal. If we are honest, we realize our hearts, our minds, and our actions are in direct opposition to our Creator.

In the gospel of Matthew, Jesus says what would have been seen as a ridiculously depressing statement. He says, "For I tell you, unless your righteousness exceeds that of the scribes and

Pharisees, you will never enter the kingdom of heaven."[2] This statement would have floored the crowds. I can just see them looking at each other whispering, "He can't be serious! Did he really just say that? That can't be true! The Pharisees are the most religiously devout and righteous people on earth. How can we be better than them?"

Pharisees were varsity. They were the best. They were the Navy SEALs of religion. And Jesus still says not even their righteousness will cut it. Because Jesus made it crystal clear that even though they might have been externally righteous, their hearts were like the inside of a filthy cup.

From a logical standpoint, do we really want to base eternity on how we look compared to someone else? That doesn't seem to be a reliable standard on which to base my entire life and eternity. Besides, isn't it tiring always comparing ourselves to others? We do it not only morally but socially, economically, and in a ton of other ways as well. It's exhausting. One of my favorite things about following Jesus is I get to drop the act, admit I'm not good enough, walk in freedom—and that's good news.

## THE GOOD NEWS OF EVERYONE BEING BAD

I can still smell the stale goldfish crackers and chalkboard dust in the old classroom I headed to most Sunday mornings. I remember sitting in my orange plastic chair, wearing my knockoff Boy Scout uniform, and listening to the lady up front with glasses tell me about the Bible by moving around the little characters in robes on the felt board. Week after week I would sit and listen as she talked about the classic Old Testament heroes like David, Noah, Abraham, Adam, and Jonah. I remember thinking places in the Bible sounded so cute based on her stories. I was—and still am—a highly visual learner, but I couldn't grasp what the world looked like all those centuries ago.

Like any kid with heroes, I wanted to be there. I wanted to smell the same air David smelled. I wanted to be on the boat with Noah. Then I saw the movie *Pleasantville* in middle school and it pretty much summed up my view of the Bible at that time. Everyone lived in black-and-white, no one got hurt, no one swore, and everything seemed perfect. I remember watching it and thinking, *That seems just like the Bible I've been learning about!*

When I finally started to read the Bible for myself at age nineteen, I was shocked—if not terrified—by the stories. Part of me felt a little angry, and part of me felt deceived that the reality of the Bible had been so glossed over. In Sunday school I was taught to be like all the "heroes" in the Old Testament, but when I reread their stories, I noticed many of them had dents in their armor.

The more I read, the more I felt the Bible looked a lot more like the movie *300* than the movie *Pleasantville*. For example, how come in Sunday school, Noah's ark was always portrayed as this happy getaway, with the sun shining and rainbows everywhere? Why on earth did people put that event on paint ings and hang them above their fireplaces? They made it look more like a Carnival cruise vacation than the outpouring of God's wrath that it was. If someone were to portray the scene in a movie or painting accurately, it would probably be rated *R*.

I can only imagine the sound of millions of people drowning: kids yelling for their moms as they sank beneath the water, people's skulls splitting open on rocks as the roaring waters tossed them around like rag dolls. I don't think the balcony of the ark was a place where Noah would go to have a fruity drink. Not too many people find it relaxing to stare at thousands of decaying corpses floating all around. I still shudder when I picture what took place.

God sent the Flood because he was sorry he even made us. The book of Genesis says, "The LORD saw that the wickedness of man was great in the earth, and that every intention of the thoughts of his heart was only evil continually. And the LORD regretted that he had made man on the earth, and it grieved him to his heart."[3]

Noah and the Flood wasn't the only story in the Bible that was not rated *G*. The ancient texts are filled with adul tery, murder, rape, incest, drunkenness, lying, deception, and betrayal—most of those by the "heroes" too. Many of the psalms were written as laments—David wrote out of a sense of angst and depression. Lot (Abraham's nephew) got drunk, had sex with his two daughters, and got them pregnant. David's son Amnon raped his half-sister Tamar and then later was killed by his half-brother Absalom. In the book of Judges, a holy man killed his mistress, chopped her up into twelve different pieces, and sent her to different parts of Israel.[4] And historically, little Hebrew boys couldn't read Song of Songs until they reached a certain age. Some of it was too explicit, sexual, and provocative.

I became mesmerized—and sometimes uncomfortable—when reading the unsanitized stories of the Bible. This seemed closer to real life than what I learned in Sunday school. It shocked me to learn that

Adam was a coward and did nothing to defend his
   wife.
Noah was a drunk.
King David committed adultery and then, to cover it
   up, had the woman's husband murdered.

Now the Bible was getting interesting. I could identify with the characters for once. Growing up, I thought the Bible was just a nice moral code for how to live life. It was boring and inaccessible. I mean, I loved some of the stories and enjoyed the Proverbs and Psalms, but sometimes they just didn't seem relevant. God seemed angry, Jesus seemed nonexistent, and all the genealogies and measurements gave me a headache. But when I started to see just how messy, just how gritty, and just how explicit the Scriptures truly are, that's when they came alive. I started to realize I wasn't the hero, nor did God want me to be.

That's how you can spot the religious people: they insist they are the heroes. They have to save the day. They have to have enough verses memorized. They have to get a new badge on their Sunday school sash. They have to defend God. This problem isn't new. In fact, Jesus dealt with the very same thing. To the religious leaders in John 5, Jesus says, "You search the Scriptures because you think that in them you have eternal life; and it is they that bear witness about me, yet you refuse to come to me that you may have life."[5]

Jesus says you can read the Bible as a checklist, but if you do, you miss the whole point.

God doesn't just give us points for trying hard. He wants us to approach him rightly. Thinking you can earn eternal life by just reading the Bible a lot is like staring at the windshield while driving, hoping you'll get where you want to go. The windshield isn't there to be looked *at*; it is designed to be looked *through*.

That's what it's like with the Bible. It was not given to us so that we could highlight and underline our way into eternity, but in hopes that we would have a special encounter with our Creator. Jesus is quite clear: We are not at the center of the Scriptures. He is. Jesus essentially says that the entire Old Testament is about him. That's quite the claim from a homeless dude who was rumored to be illegitimate!

When I started to understand this, many of the Sunday school stories began to make sense. I saw them as less about great heroes I should aspire to be like, and more about great failures that Jesus works through. Every character, every story, every construction plan—I still don't know what a cubit is, by the way—is a shadow or a symbol of Jesus. This is good news, because if we aren't the heroes, we can stop trying to save the day. Let me give you three examples, or stories, in which we typically miss Jesus entirely.

## Jonah

"Jonah and the Whale" is a classic sanitized children's Bible story. He was famously swallowed up by a whale and lived in its stomach three days for disobeying God. But let's back up for those who maybe don't know the story or have heard it told differently.

Jonah was a guy who knew God. He was a prophet called to speak to people on God's behalf. One day God asked Jonah to tell the people in the city of Nineveh about him. When you read *Nineveh*, think *Vegas*. Sin city. Rebellion. Debauchery. So when God told him to go to Nineveh, he had a "Whatchu talkin' 'bout, Willis?" moment. He refused. He thought they didn't deserve redemption, so he jumped on a ship and sailed in the exact opposite direction. God continued to pursue and pull at Jonah, and he sent a storm to get his attention. The other sailors on the boat knew something was up and finally threw Jonah overboard at Jonah's request. He knew the storm was because of him. Immediately, the storms calmed and a fish—not a whale—swallowed Jonah whole. He was stuck in its belly for three days.[6]

Commonly we tell the story as if it's about us—that is, we don't want to be like Jonah who disobeys God and gets thrown into the sea. But the story takes on a whole new meaning when looking for Jesus. When you read it, contrast Jonah's actions with Jesus' actions. Jonah turned his back on the people of Nineveh, thinking they weren't worthy of God's love; but Jesus came to save us, knowing we aren't worthy but loving us still. Jonah lived in the belly of a fish for three days—for being disobedient—and saved a shipload of crewmen; but Jesus lived in the belly of the earth for three days (though he was perfectly obedient) and saved humanity from death.

Jonah isn't about Jonah.
Jonah isn't about us.
Jonah is about Jesus.

## Cain and Abel

Cain and Abel were the first sons of Adam and Eve. These two brothers were charged with bringing an offering to God, and the Scriptures say Abel brought one that God had "regard for," but God despised the one Cain brought.[7] Usually this is the only part of the story we hear in church. We are told we must bring a sacrifice God asks for, not one we think he will like. This is true but not the entire story.

Because God didn't like Cain's sacrifice, Cain got angry and killed his brother Abel out of wicked jealousy. Abel's blood was "crying . . . from the ground" for justice and the guilt of Cain.

Now contrast Abel's blood with Jesus' blood: Abel's blood called for Cain's guilt, while Jesus' blood calls for our acquittal. We have all been like Cain, committing hateful murder and even killing God himself. While the blood is on our hands, Jesus' perfect sacrifice calls out for our innocence. Free to go. Not guilty. That's God's verdict. Perfect, spotless, blameless, and holy, even though we killed the Son of God.

That's grace, and it's free, because it cost him everything.

## David and Goliath

David was the little shepherd boy who killed the giant warrior Goliath with a stone and slingshot, right?[8] I can't remember the number of times I heard in Sunday school, "If you just have faith like David, you can kill giants in your life!" I was told this over and over again. If I just have enough faith, then I can stop looking at porn. If I just have enough faith, I can stop getting angry. The problem was, this just didn't seem to work. I'd muster up all the faith I had. I'd pray and tell God this time was different. I'd quote Scripture to myself when being tempted. But no matter what I did, when my giants—lust, pride, self-righteousness—fell down, I would walk over, take their pulse, and they would just get back up and beat the crap out of me.

I kept trying to be like David, but I kept realizing I can't actually be David. I was trying to play the wrong character in the story. There are three characters in the story, even though we only talk about two—David and Goliath. The third character no one talks about is Israel—the spectators on the sidelines. The entire nation of Israel is sitting on the hill thinking they are all about to die. They're terrified because they see how big Goliath is, and they know how frail they are. The book of 1 Samuel says that Israel was "much afraid." We are weak, feeble, incapable Israel. That makes Jesus like David in this story.

Jesus is a better savior because while David killed Goliath—a seemingly large and terrifying opponent—Jesus killed sin—a much more dangerous and terrifying opponent. He chopped off its head, so it no longer has power. We can be honest and transparent about our sins and failures because we aren't the ones fighting. Jesus fought for us. This is good news because it means we are free to be messed up. If we are Israel, then let's play that character well. Be honest about your weakness, be honest that you're scared, and be honest about the fact that it's Jesus who defeats the sins that trip you up, not you. God cast us as Israel, not the hero.

Both David and Jesus used unlikely means to defeat the enemy. David had only speed and a slingshot; Jesus defeated sin by being meek, humble, and murdered rather than through tyrannical political reign as everyone thought he would.

His ways aren't our ways, but his ways save. Our ways don't.

This is why it's good news we aren't good enough. There is something so tough about grace, though, that some people refuse to accept it. Other world religions or worldviews make ladders we need to climb to get to heaven, when the real

Christian faith can only be lived by army crawling to get it. We have to get low. We have to humble ourselves. And I promise joy is on the other side.

The paradox of the Scripture is that it calls us way more sinful than we think we are, and it calls us way more loved than we think we are. Many people can't get their minds around grace, and they try to convince themselves that they are fine, that they can make it, and that they are good enough. I know this line of reasoning all too well, as this is how I thought for many years. But our hearts don't like it. We know that "good enough" is relative. It keeps whispering our inadequacies. And if that isn't enough, calling out evil can turn on us. Sometimes we will say things like genocide, murder, and adultery are evil. But even in doing that we are appealing to some form of a standard that could turn on us also.

And so let's be done with the comparison game. Let's be done with constantly fighting for the higher moral ground to stand on and look down on everyone else. Let's be done with thinking we can actually earn something that is impossible to earn. Let's stop trying to be perfect and righteous because those are not the people God is looking for. God is looking for people who can admit their needs and surrender to a Savior, because if the Bible is any indication, it doesn't matter how messed up you are. If you love him, he can and will use you.

1. Have you ever thought God grades on a curve? Why?
2. Many times we are more concerned with the outward appearance of our lives than the internal transformation of them. Describe a person in your life for whom this isn't true.
3. Jeff contrasts seeing the Bible as a moral code and seeing it as a collection of gritty, real-life stories. Why does the Bible sometimes get sanitized for public consumption?
4. What is your favorite story from the Old Testament? How does it point to Jesus?
5. Jeff writes that "we are free to be messed up" and don't need to fight sin on our own because of God's grace. Do you agree? Why or why not?
6. What's your relationship with the Bible?

# CHAPTER 6

# RELIGION IS THE MEANS TO GET THINGS FROM GOD / IF WE SEEK JESUS, WE GET GOD

Growing up, it was just my mom and me. I have two sisters, but they were raised by my dad, and I was raised by my mom. As with most custody cases, we did the typical every-other-weekend thing where we'd swap. To be honest, I never thought too much of it. As a kid, you just take things as they are. It seemed normal, especially because in the neighborhoods where I grew up in the Tacoma area, it was rare to see a family with a mom and dad.

Looking back, I wouldn't change a thing about my upbringing. It made me who I am today, and I'm thankful for how those experiences have shaped me. Today my entire family lives within a few miles of each other, and we get along great. I love my dad, mom, and two sisters so much. When I was growing up, though, we certainly had our issues.

When I was eleven years old, one of my sisters moved in with my mom and me. Because of my mom's mental hardship and physical disability, we didn't have a lot of money. We were living in a tiny two-bedroom house in a low-income area. When my sister moved in, we didn't have much room or money to accommodate another person, so we had to make it work. Because my sister was older and a girl, my mom gave her the bedroom. My sister was just entering high school at the time, and so sharing with her younger brother wasn't an option. Even though we were siblings, we had never lived together. This was a big transition.

Looking back, I see it was my mom's way of making my sister feel welcome and offering her what she had at my dad's house. Since there were not many places to go, I put my mattress on the floor in the hallway and used that as my bedroom for the next couple of years. It really wasn't that bad. I was clothed. I was fed. And I had a mattress to sleep on every night. But on more than a few occasions I remember praying, "God, where are you? If you love me so much, why do we struggle? Why can we barely buy groceries? How come all my friends have nice houses and everything they want, and I'm stuck sleeping in the hallway?"

To be honest, I wasn't praying that prayer out of sheer pain. I was flat-out embarrassed. I was just entering middle school, where a lot of changes start to happen. The entire structure of middle school was different from elementary. Everyone seemed to care about everything, and it was the first time I felt the aching pressure to fit in. How I dressed, how I spoke, and how good I was at things were highlighted and scrutinized. I felt awkward and embarrassed by having to sleep in a hallway.

*What would my friends think?*
*Would they still accept me?*
*Would I get made fun of?*

I still remember the pressure of those thoughts.

At that time I had a vague concept of God. As an eleven-year-old, I didn't see how God was any different from Santa Claus: I would ask for something and hope he came through. So I'd lie in bed at night wondering why, if he loved me so much, I didn't have a bedroom. It feels trivial caring that much about it now, but that thought led to a real apathy toward God.

He must be uninterested in me, because if he was interested, wouldn't he prove it? Why did my mom struggle so much? Why did we have to rely on food stamps to pay for our groceries? Why did we move so much? Why couldn't we afford the baseball equipment when some of my friends got whatever they asked for? It was as if God was an eternal slot machine; and if nothing was coming out, then he didn't love me.

## TWISTING THE BIBLE

When I was younger, I thought God's favor on me, my sister, and my mom was solely displayed by our physical and earthly possessions. I thought if I was good, God owed me something. To make it worse, whenever I turned on the TV, the preacher with the ten-thousand-dollar suit usually told me the same thing. It wasn't until years later when I was in college and just starting to dig into the Scriptures that I realized this was one of religion's biggest lies.

In the parable of the rich young ruler, the young man didn't want *God*; he just wanted what God could *give* him.[1] Many Christians don't really care about God; they just want to use him to get what they truly want—status, a nice job, a car, forgiveness—you name it. Even the benefits of a relationship with God—forgiveness, love, redemption, grace, etc.—can be elevated to the place of God if we are more concerned with getting those things rather than seeing those things as an avenue to God. Rather than God being God, we turn ourselves into God and make him our prostitute. We are just the pimps who make all the rules, run the show, and only call on him when we need him to do a job. He does what we say. All we have to do is "sow a seed of faith" or take a few scriptures that talk about "blessing" completely out of context and we will live a good and abundant life.

I've heard many of these so-called pastors quote, "For you know the grace of our Lord Jesus Christ, that though he was rich, yet for your sake he became poor, so that you by his poverty might become rich."[2] They'll then proceed to make the argument that we are to be rich because Jesus humbled himself. They completely miss the context: Paul is talking about spiritual riches, not financial riches. Jesus was rich in spiritual inheritance in heaven, but put that aside to come rescue us. And we were poor and feeble and sin-sick, but Jesus gave us the inheritance that he left, which is every spiritual blessing in the heavenly places.[3]

I've also heard people quote, "Beloved, I pray that all may go well with you and that you may be in good health, as it goes well with your soul."[4] So according to some preachers, if you are in bad health, you are in sin. But that verse has John praying that it "may" go well with us in our health, and that it certainly goes well with us in our souls. That's the difference. Our souls are anchored when we have Jesus, and we can and should pray for health and vitality; but if that is not present, we know the anchor is still there regardless. The blessing and the prosperity of God are invisible and spiritual, not financial or physical.

One of the most dangerous things about the Bible is that it is big enough to say whatever we want it to say if we are willing to remove the context. Want to have sex with your girlfriend before you're married? I'm sure there is a verse on love in the Bible you could twist to justify that. Want to get a convenient divorce because you don't feel like serving your spouse? I once heard someone argue that "God wants us to prosper," and since he didn't like his spouse anymore, the marriage wasn't of God. He completely disregarded the multiple explicit teachings of Jesus to the contrary. Want to live in lavish luxury, hoarding all your possessions and wealth, and call it God "blessing you"? There's plenty of literature you can find on that.

The most dangerous thing about the human heart is that we want to reverse the roles by making God the responder and us the initiators. We make ourselves into God, and we make God a beggar. We look on him the same way some of us sadly look upon the homeless community—with contempt, at our whim, and incapable without our help. We initiate, and he responds. But the Bible is exactly the opposite.

Jesus is Lord; we are not.
Jesus is King; we are not.
Jesus is Savior; we are not.

The best part is that this is good news. Only when we humbly call on God to speak into our lives—knowing if he doesn't, we won't succeed—are we actually in a safe place.

When it comes to the marks of God's favor on our lives, prosperity preachers and some Christians distort the

Scriptures. They tell us that if something is going wrong in our lives, it must be because of sin. If we want to be healed, if we want to have a nice house, if we want to get rid of our struggles, then all we have to do is have enough faith. But if a life without hardship shows the favor of God, then God must have been very angry at Jesus, Paul, Job, and others.

Crucified?

Thrown in prison?

Shipwrecked?

Diseased?

Either God hated them or they had a lot of sin. My eleven-year-old self sleeping in the hallway had nothing on them.

## DESIRING THE GIFTS OVER THE GIVER

By our nature we all pursue and desire everything outside of God. We all have elevated the gifts above the Giver. We all have taken the creation over the Creator. Most of the things we elevate aren't inherently evil. In fact, they are good. But our *distortions* of those things are evil. To get a good view of why we are here and what everything was created for, we have to go back to the Creation story.

In the book of Genesis, God creates everything: plants, trees, birds, seas, sun, planets, *everything*. And then he creates Adam and Eve, puts them in the garden, and tells them to "work it and keep it."[5] Every day after he created something, God declared that what he created was "good." He doesn't say it is evil. He doesn't say it is "secular."

He says it is *good*.

All of it.

That means God created sex. And he declared it to be good. Of course, this is in the context of the marriage covenant, but in that context, sex is beautiful and wonderful. I know some religious types have completely written off sex as dirty, evil, gross, or not for "godly" people. If anything, it's simply for procreation, but not to be enjoyed. I know Christian girls in particular struggle after hearing that sex is sinful or gross their entire lives and then are expected to just turn on the it's-awesome-now switch once they get married. Does that shock anyone else? It's not as if sex was our idea. It was God's. We didn't think it up. God didn't place Adam and Eve naked in a garden and then come back a few hours later yelling at Adam to get off of his wife and put his clothes back on.

It's important for us to understand fully that sex, as well as other things like vocation, politics, art, music, and pleasure, aren't evil. After all, God said they were good! But they don't define us, they aren't markings of God's favor, and they can be distorted. Seeing monetary gain as evidence of God's love is nothing new, though it has significantly rooted in American soil recently. But we also need to not slam it so hard we end up on the other side of the aisle doing the same thing, just dressed in different clothes.

There is this weird strain of Christianity going around that seems to have done just that: if you aren't poor, if you aren't giving away all you have, then you aren't a good Christian. The problem is still the same. These Christians are also defining worth with God by external behavior and standing. That's not good or helpful. Everything is God's; we are stewards who have it on loan as gifts from him, and we should use his gifts to build his kingdom, not our own. Some he gives more than others, but we can't measure ourselves by what we have or don't have. We can only measure ourselves by the fact that we love and know Jesus.

## CREATED FOR HIM

I still remember Alyssa's and my first kiss. It was exactly what you'd expect. Completely awkward. Completely uncomfortable. And completely epic. You better believe I fist-pumped right after. I also still remember the first time we held hands, the first time we hugged, and the first time we said, "I love you." Call me sentimental—or maybe it's just the fact I remember a lot of things—but they were all incredible and meaningful to me. The cool part about us getting married is that I get to kiss her and hold her hand whenever I want for the rest of our lives. Those things are great benefits of us being together. But here's the thing: they aren't the *essence* of us being together.

I think too many times as Christians, we confuse benefits with essence. We pursue the *benefits* of a relationship rather than the *essence* of that relationship. This trade-off is terrible because only when you pursue a relationship rightly can you enjoy its gifts. When you pursue the benefits, they never seem to satisfy, and you miss out on it all. I really like the way the author C. S. Lewis said it: "Put first things first and we get second things thrown in: put second things first and we lose both first and second things. We never get, say, even the sensual pleasure of food at its best when we are being greedy."[6]

Sometimes the game of life is like a bait and switch: something lures us in, we bite, and it doesn't satisfy. We think, *What happened? I thought that thing promised satisfaction?* The problem is because nothing can sustain the weight of itself. Everything self-terminates the minute it becomes self-focused.

Eat food for the sake of eating food, and it'll never satisfy.

Eat food for the sake of nourishment, and give thanks to God for creating food, and it strangely begins to satisfy.

Am I the only one who's been caught in this cycle hundreds, if not thousands, of times? We short-circuit whenever we pursue the benefits and not the essence because it's God's way of getting our attention and showing us he's the true satisfaction. God wants us to pursue him *first.*

This is why the religion that spews a false gospel and turns God into Santa Claus is so damnable. It's putting second things first, which is just a different way of saying *idolatry.* When you concentrate on God, you can actually enjoy his gifts in a meaningful way. But when you pursue just the gifts themselves, they become the product of despair rather than joy.

How weird would it be if a father gave his son a Christmas present, and immediately after opening it the boy ran into his room, locked the door, and didn't come out for days because he was too busy playing with the gift? He'd not only get sick of it quickly but also disappoint his father by not saying thank you. Gifts are meant to draw out thankfulness to another person. It's like that with God too. When the son receives the gift as exactly that, a gift, he thanks his father and enjoys it to the fullest because he's not a slave to it. But if he runs to the gift itself, he will be disappointed. He's putting a demand on that gift that it cannot sustain.

So what do you pursue—gifts or essence? Blessings or intimacy? Let's go back to my relationship with Alyssa. If the main reason I married her was for the physical benefits, then when those are not there or are unavailable, I will get angry, lose my joy, or leave. For example, if one of us has the flu, it's not wise to have close contact until the bug is gone. Those seasons of sickness highlight why I really married her. If I'm disproportionally upset, it shows the driving force in our relationship is the benefits, not her. But if I married her just to be with her—the essence of her, not just the benefits for me to enjoy—then even if she is sick, has a physical accident that changes her appearance, or becomes paralyzed, I'm content because I still have *her*. By putting my stock in our relationship in just the essence of who she is rather than what she gives, I am ultimately putting my stock in something way stronger than the other. What she gives can be taken away or shifted quickly, but outside of death, who she is can't be.

That's how it works with God. When we understand he is our ultimate goal, then we find a joy and a power that starts to resemble New Testament Christianity. If, however, we put our hope, faith, and worth in what God gives, then what happens when those things disappear or leave? That's when people say, "I tried God. He didn't work for me." Usually the truth is they tried to *use* God, and it didn't work for them. Even beautiful things such as forgiveness, clear conscience, joy in life, and adoption into the family of God are all benefits of *being* a Christian, but not the ultimate goal.

All those benefits are meant to open the possibility of living in unbroken intimacy with our Creator for the rest of time. His face, and his face alone, needs to be the driving force of our lives. If it's not, we are worshiping something else, and sooner or later that idol will be taken from us by a trial, circumstance, or death.

In the New Testament, the apostle Peter said, "For Christ also suffered once for sins, the righteous for the unrighteous, that he might bring us to God."[7] He says Jesus suffered and exchanged places with us to bring us to God. It doesn't say to bring us to a new Bentley. It doesn't say to give us health and wealth. It doesn't say to bring us worldly blessings. It says he died to bring us to *himself.* How awesome is that? We were created for God.

Saint Augustine also came to this realization by famously praying, "You have made us for yourself, and our hearts are restless until they rest in you."[8]

How amazing is it that God actually gives us himself? The infinite, glorious, spectacular, and altogether lovely God of the universe is all ours. We can exhaust money. We can exhaust sex. We can exhaust our jobs. But we can't exhaust God. He gives us the one thing that will never run out, never get old, and never fail: himself!

In addition, God makes it clear in the Bible that he is the only thing that can't be taken from us.

My job can be taken.

My health can be taken.

My ability to type and write can be taken.

But my identity as a child of God can never be taken.

## HAVING JOY DESPITE CIRCUMSTANCES

As long as we have the presence of an infinite loving God, we can do anything, even when our world is in chaos. It's that power that looks strange to others. A nonbeliever doesn't think twice when we praise God for giving us Bentleys, but they do think twice when we get evicted from our homes and still praise God. Having joy in God not because of circumstances but despite circumstances is what makes God look great—and it's a true joy that comes from within.

The thing that most bothers me about the Santa Claus–Jesus Christianity is it completely mocks some of the most powerful testimonies of God's grace. I can think of one story in particular in the persecuted church that makes me tear up every time I hear it. In Nik Ripken's book *The Insanity of God*, he details many stories of people facing trials and hardships through persecution. Some are executed, some are tortured, and some are beaten. Somehow these Christians still seem to hold strong—and in most cases, their faith strengthens! God is most glorified in our lives when we show him to be most glorious regardless of what is thrown our way.

The story I'm thinking of that shows this so beautifully is about a man named Dmitri who fell in love with Jesus during the communist reign in Russia. Shortly after becoming a follower of Jesus, he opened his house to others to talk about Jesus, sing songs, and read the Bible. Quickly many people began to come. So many came, in fact, that the government noticed, and he was fired from his job. Still Dmitri continued to preach and read the Bible to others in his home. That's when it got real interesting.

One night when he was holding church in his house, soldiers broke in. One grabbed Dmitri, slapped him around, and said, "We have warned you, and warned you, and warned you. I will not warn you again! If you do not stop this nonsense, this is the least that is going to happen to you." As Nik Ripkin describes: "The officer pushed his way back toward the door, a small grandmother took her life in her hands, stepped out of the anonymity of that worshiping community, and waved a finger in the officer's face. Sounding like an Old Testament prophet, she declared, 'You have laid hands on a man of God and you will NOT survive!'"[9]

I want that old lady as my grandma—or my private security detail. There's one thing I know for certain, and it's that you don't mess with an old lady on fire for Jesus. And she was totally right! Two days later the officer died of a heart attack. At the next meeting 150 people showed up, so Dmitri was thrown into jail for seventeen years.

He was separated from his family, his kids, and other believers. He endured torture, mocking, and beatings. He was the only believer among fifteen hundred hardened criminals. Dmitri noted that separation from the body of Christ was actually more painful than the physical torture he endured in prison. The guards just couldn't seem to break him. Every single day for seventeen years, he would wake up, stand up, raise his arms in praise to God, and then sing a particular song to Jesus. The same song, every day. While he would sing, the other prisoners would laugh, curse at him, and sometimes even throw human waste at him to get him to stop.

Whenever Dmitri would find a scrap of paper, he would sneak it back to his cell. He would write as many Bible verses as he could remember on those pieces of paper, and when they were filled he would stick them to a concrete pillar in the corner of his cell. He called them "praise offerings" to God. Whenever guards saw him, they would come into his cell, take the papers, and beat him severely. Still, he never stopped. For seventeen years he never stopped.

At one point, when the guards finally had enough and saw he couldn't be broken, they decided to execute him. As he was being taken away, fifteen hundred inmates began to sing the same song they had heard Dmitri sing every morning and raised their arms to Jesus.

Dmitri's jailers instantly released their hold on his arms and stepped away from him in terror.

One of them demanded to know, "Who are you?" Dmitri straightened his back and stood as tall and as proud as he could.

He responded: "I am a son of the Living God, and Jesus is his name!"[10]

Dmitri was released shortly after that and returned to his family. Such a beautiful story of true faith, heartache, trials, and glorifying Jesus in any circumstance! But what gave Dmitri that power? Honestly ask yourself, what sustained him in such brutal circumstances? Was it someone telling him not to drink beer or get tattoos? Was it the idea that if he stayed faithful in prison, God would reward him with money? The thing that made Dmitri so powerful was that he saw the presence of God *as* the reward.

Even in prison.

Even when fellow prisoners were throwing their fecal
matter at him.

Even while he was tortured.

He knew that intimacy with his Creator was what he was created for, and if he had that, then he could go through anything. This is what it comes down to:

Jesus doesn't promise us worldly *success*; he promises
*himself.*

Jesus doesn't promise us *riches*; he promises a rich
life *in him.*

Jesus doesn't promise us *easy lives*; he promises to be
*with us.*

Before I was a Christian, it was hard for me to grasp that God's love isn't gauged by earthly circumstances. I completely relate to those who are asking, "If God can't give us earthly blessings, why should we follow him?" My answer now, as a Christian, is that God is worth it. We all desire to be known, loved, and seen for who we truly are. Most of those tangible or social goals such as money, power, and relationships seem to be one step ahead of us. Should we reach them, those things never deliver the feeling of self-worth we expect to gain from them. We are nothing but slaves to the next goal. We might be able to choose our slave master, but we are slaves nonetheless.

The unique thing about Jesus is that he gives us security. We can be sick, we can be healthy, we can be rich, we can be poor; but if we have Jesus, we have rest. One of my favorite verses in the New Testament is in the book of Ephesians: "Blessed be the God and Father of our Lord Jesus Christ, who has blessed us in Christ with every spiritual blessing in the heavenly places."[11]

Paul reminds us we don't need every physical blessing because we already have every spiritual blessing.

We don't need financial security because we have spiritual security.

We don't need physical health because we have spiritual health.

And the best part, he says, is that those blessings are in the *heavenly* places.

When I was younger I was a punk, and I'd steal things from my friends. Immediately after stealing something, I'd hide it back at home in my dresser. When my friends saw me the next day, they'd tackle me and start searching, but I would always chuckle when they started to search for their stuff because I knew whatever I had stolen wasn't on me. It was secure somewhere else. It was back home where nothing could touch it.

Our security in Jesus is similar to that—except not only do we not have to steal it, but it's given to us for free. Our blessings and security are in the heavenly places where no one can touch or taint them. They are right next to God Almighty and far away from sin and death.

So when death or sin or trial or suffering comes, we can smile because our lives are hidden with Christ in God.[12] It's not here on earth, but has already been achieved and given. You find a person who truly believes this, and you'll find a person who can't be touched. He or she may be bruised, beat up, and hurt by this life, but nothing can reach his or her life because it isn't even here.

1. Describe a time when you thought of God as Santa Claus.
2. Contrast a spiritual richness with a financial richness. Which one is more natural for you to recognize when you think about God's blessing in your life? Why?
3. Jeff writes that at times we confuse the essence of something with the benefits of it. Has this happened to you in your experience of Christianity? What is the essence of following Jesus for you?
4. How do you respond to the idea that God cannot be exhausted, that God is the only thing in your life that will never run out?
5. "Jesus doesn't promise us easy lives; he promises to be with us." How do you respond to this?
6. Can you follow Jesus even if that means not achieving success as it's defined by modern American culture? Why or why not?

# WITH RELIGION, IF YOU ARE SUFFERING, GOD IS PUNISHING YOU / GOD ALREADY PUNISHED JESUS ON YOUR BEHALF, SO SUFFERING IS HIS MERCY

At the end of my freshman year in college, I moved back home after a year in San Diego. I had just started following

Jesus and wanted a fresh start, fewer distractions, and more baseball. I thought going home for my sophomore year would be a time of immense growth and victory, but it didn't turn out that way. It was one of the hardest years of my life. My sin was tripping me up, I couldn't seem to change, and my world started to fall apart when my girlfriend broke up with me.

One day in particular in the fall semester of my sophomore year, I was lying on the bed completely drained. I wasn't tired from physical exertion; I was tired from emotional pain. You ever had that? It's weird how when emotional pain is sharp enough, it almost feels like it physically hurts. For weeks I couldn't sleep—but the funny thing is, all I wanted to do *was* sleep. Sleeping was the only time I didn't feel depressed or burdened. It was the only time the pain disappeared. It was about lunchtime, and I had finished class and crashed on the bed. That's when everything flooded over me. It was in that moment I had a scary but very concise thought. *The easiest way to take away this pain would be to put myself out of my misery.*

*Huh? Did I just think that?* I thought only super-depressed people had those thoughts. I snapped back into reality, shocked I even had that thought. What was more shocking was how *attractive* the thought was. It was a whisper that promised something it couldn't give—peace.

Over the next few weeks, the thought came back to haunt me. Usually I settled for just falling asleep, but my need to escape the pain was becoming unbearable. How could a breakup be serious enough to rock me so badly? How come

I couldn't just get over it? Why did it feel like my world was crashing down? Why couldn't I be honest with this pain? Why did I care what others would think? The wound felt too raw and too vulnerable to bring it to light.

I didn't know then, but looking back I can see that I had made my relationship an idol in my life. It was my functional god.

I didn't just like my girlfriend; I *worshiped* her.

She wasn't just my girlfriend; she was my *god*.

My worth, my identity, and my satisfaction were all wrapped up in her, and when I lost control of the situation and control of her, it felt like my god was being taken from me. That's the truth with any idol—it will rock you to your core when it leaves. When a good thing leaves you, it might make you sad. But when an ultimate thing leaves you, you feel like you can't live anymore.

And that's what happened to me. For the next few months, I hated life. I saw no reason to live and just went through the motions, all the while putting on a smile. And this whole time I was just months into my new relationship with Jesus. I had just started to read the Bible and pray again.

I remember reading the Bible one morning during this time, and I'd had enough. I grabbed my Bible and threw it against the wall. I shouted, "This doesn't even work! If you are so loving and so good, why does my life suck? I've been good and I've obeyed. And if anything, stuff has gotten worse since I started following you!"

What happened next shocked me, and I still have a hard time describing it. While it wasn't audible, something outside of me spoke, something I would have never thought up myself: "Now that you've decided to be honest, we can finally get somewhere."

My heart was too busy drowning in pride, however. *How dare God repay me like this? How dare he let all these bad things happen to me? I was good. He owes me!* I was standing there cursing God with the very vocal cords he had created. The fact that I was even breathing at that moment was his grace all over me. It hit me even harder when I started to look at seemingly ungodly people and see how great their lives were. I immediately decided to run to God with my complaint. *God, why do they have such nice lives, and they don't even serve you? That's not fair!*

Again I heard that inaudible voice: "If you want fair, you'd be in hell."

*Ouch.*

It was the truth, though. None of us deserve life. It's all a gift. If we wanted true justice, none of us would be here. It puts a whole new perspective on life when you realize even the ability to get out of bed in the morning is a wonderful extension of grace by our Creator. Thankfulness is the quickest path to joy. He owes us *nothing*, but he gives us *everything*.

## WHERE IS GOD WHEN IT HURTS?

Sooner or later life will hit you. And it will hit you hard. Your mom gets cancer, you don't get into the school you wanted to get into, and the girl or guy you thought was "the one" leaves. It's in those moments we all wonder, *Where is God? Where is a loving God in the middle of this pain?*

The question continued to haunt me. How come the preachers I heard growing up all told me if I came to Jesus, he would make my life better? No more pain. No more suffering. For me, if anything, things got worse. My failures started to haunt me, I couldn't seem to stop doing things I now knew were wrong, I felt guilty all the time, and relationships and circumstances in my life were falling apart. *So much for my best life now.*

I'm only starting to get a glimpse of God's redemption in the midst of suffering. In this world pain is inevitable, and sometimes it's one of the only things that can help us grow.

When I travel, I love hearing all the stereotypes about Seattle: "Does everyone just drink coffee all day and wear flannels?" No, not everyone. We don't let kids have coffee until age five.

"Isn't everyone a hippie in Seattle?" There are at least two people on my block who aren't hippies.

The one I hear most often is, "Doesn't it rain there all year?" The answer is no, you foolish foreigners. Not even close. It only rains ten months out of the year.

I've also heard, "It's really pretty out there! Everything is really green." That one is actually true.

There is no place on earth I'd rather be in the summer than Seattle. The mountains, the trees, the lakes, the rivers—it is truly amazing. It averages between seventy and eighty degrees with a cool breeze, so you can actually be outside and not die of heatstroke. Whenever I travel to the south during July or August, I feel like Satan is breathing down my back the minute I step off the plane. Feeling like I'm about to pass out is not my ideal summer.

Seattle truly is a beautiful place. But that beauty comes at a cost. What makes it so green? What makes it so fresh? What makes the foliage so vast and fruitful?

The answer is *rain*.

Seattle wouldn't look like Seattle without it. The months that suck fuel the months that are awesome. Without the rain there is no beauty in the summer. Rain gives depth, it gives beauty, and it gives roots. If a plant is only exposed to sun and no rain, it becomes dry, flimsy, and dead.

Too many times we curse the rain in our lives—suffering, trials, hardships—but the truth is, without rain nothing grows. Without rain there's no fruit—just dry, flaky, and nasty leaves. Sometimes suffering is actually God's blessing rather than God's curse. It is clear in Scripture that he is not the source of evil, nor did he cause it, but he promises he can use it.[1]

The story of Joseph is one of the most famous examples. He was sold into Egyptian slavery by his brothers. He then found favor with the Egyptian authorities and over the years climbed the ranks to become the second most powerful man next to Pharoah. Because of this, when a famine hit Egypt, Joseph was the only one who could help. When his brothers came to Egypt to get grain, Joseph not only sent them back with an abundance but also put their money back into their money sacks.

Joseph being sold into slavery was horrible.

Joseph being thrown into prison for things he didn't do was horrible.

But God used it.

Suffering is never from God, but he can redeem it. What better example is there than the murder and crucifixion of his own Son? The world intended it for evil and saw Jesus as a failure, but God used it to bring good and actually brought down the forces of evil in that moment. He can see the whole picture.

We know what we *want*; but he knows what we *need*.

He gives even though we think he's taking. And when God does that, he is beautifully shaping you and molding you into the image of his Son. If everything were always awesome in our lives, we wouldn't see vital growth. The seasons when it's tough, when it hurts, and when you hate it are bringing a season of sun and a season of life.

Just wait.

It's coming.

When I'm going through a particularly tough time, I read this quote by author Elisabeth Kübler-Ross over and over again to give me hope: "The most beautiful people we have known are those who have known defeat, known suffering, known struggle, known loss, and have found their way out of the depths. These persons have an appreciation, a sensitivity, and an understanding of life that fills them with compassion, gentleness, and a deep loving concern. Beautiful people do not just happen."[2]

I love that: "Beautiful people don't just happen."

I want to be careful here, though. If a girl is raped, she should not thank God for it. A wife who lost her husband to an automobile accident should not be happy. Sometimes life hurts. Deeply. Sometimes there is no explanation.

So what do you do then? What do you do when the only thing you want to do is yell at God and tell him how awful it is? You do exactly that.

Cry.

Yell.

Scream.

Be honest.

Be transparent.

And be vulnerable.

For the first nineteen years of my life, I wanted God to give me an answer, but now I've found it is better when I just get *him*. An answer isn't going to bring that spouse back. An answer won't ease that pain. But what will is God's grace in the depths of our souls. As Christians, God doesn't promise us an easy life, but he does promise to be with us in whatever we go through. He will never leave us or forsake us.[3]

I'm not a theologian. I can't explain the problem of evil and suffering, and I can't give you an awesome formula that explains why bad things happen. But in all honesty, is an answer really what we crave? If someone legitimately answered your question about why there is evil and suffering, would you be fully satisfied? I used to think that if only I could get the right answer, then I would be content. But I realized a right answer doesn't help the pain.

> What we really want is healing.
> What we really want is intimacy.
> What we really want is not to feel alone in the hard
> times.

And those things Jesus answers. Jesus knows what life is like. He doesn't hang out in heaven and tell us to be good and moral without reaching down to us. Jesus doesn't make us come to him; he comes to us. He walks the same earth we walk. He had to deal with the same things we deal with—going hungry, relationship problems, friends dying, and friends' betrayal.

Who more could better understand just how rugged this world is than the Son of God who not only lived it himself but also let its inhabitants kill him?

## GOD IS NOT PUNISHING YOU

Because I try to make myself accessible through YouTube, e-mail, Facebook, and other forms of social media, people frequently send me messages about what they are going through. On more than one occasion I've gotten e-mails detailing sexual abuse. I can't even begin to explain the grief I feel when reading some of these stories. That topic is one of the hardest ones to encounter. One e-mail in particular was from a woman who was raped by multiple men while she was in the military. In her e-mail to me, she detailed how she hadn't shared that with anyone other than her mother. Apparently, when she told her mom, her mom replied, "When you're not right with God, bad things happen."

It's an understatement to say I was outraged when I read what her mom said.

That is pure evil and not at all helpful. God does not delight in suffering.

I use that example because I know she's not the only one something like that has happened to and received a similar response. Whether it's through TV, parents, or our thoughts, when bad stuff happens to us, we sometimes think that God is punishing us, that he must hate us or take no interest in us.

Again, when you are suffering, God is not punishing you. I am so sure of this because God promised that he has already laid all punishment on Jesus on our behalf. In fact, hundreds of years before Jesus even came, God promised he'd swallow all that up. In the Old Testament, the prophet Isaiah said,

*He was despised and rejected by men;*
   *a man of sorrows, and acquainted with grief;*
*and as one from whom men hide their faces*
   *he was despised, and we esteemed him not.*

*Surely he has borne our griefs*
   *and carried our sorrows;*
*yet we esteemed him stricken,*
   *smitten by God, and afflicted.*
*But he was pierced for our transgressions;*
   *he was crushed for our iniquities;*
*upon him was the chastisement that brought us peace,*
   *and with his wounds we are healed.*[4]

Jesus was rejected.
He was acquainted with grief.
He was despised.

The God of the universe willingly chose that path so ultimately we wouldn't have to. He blazed the trail of eternal suffering so that we wouldn't have to. In addition, he also identified with us in our physical suffering. We can see it throughout the Bible! In the Hebrew culture, God is always giving special attention to the poor, the oppressed, and the downtrodden. He says he is "Father of the fatherless and protector of widows."[5]

In the Bible, God makes it very clear that when one of his

people suffers, he suffers. When one of his people aches, he aches. When one of his people hurts, he hurts. He is so interwoven with his people that if anything is against his people, he sees it as an act against him. You are not alone.

He says again in the Psalms that he "heals the brokenhearted / and binds up their wounds."[6] Even though we might not be able to explain why bad things happen or be able to give the reason for suffering, we do know what the reason isn't:

It isn't because he doesn't love us.
It isn't because he doesn't care.
It isn't because we aren't noticed.

God doesn't give us a nice tidy answer on why suffering and evil exist, but he does blatantly and explicitly show us what the reason isn't. Knowing what Jesus did on the cross, his love is too potent and too obvious for us to say he must not care. A God who hates suffering and evil just as much as we do was willing to subject himself to it in order to reconcile us to him.

He got involved in our mess.
He got involved in our hurt.
He got involved in our pain.

And he still knows what it feels like today.

As Christians, the example Jesus set should pave the way for how we help people who are suffering. Live long enough and you will run into the sheer damage this world can impose on others. Grief. Shame. Death. Hurt. Pain. It's all around us every day. We can't escape it. This is the world we live in.

When people come to us in the midst of their pain, how dare we flippantly quote some Bible verses as if that alone would help? How dare we think we can just send them some balloons? How dare we overspiritualize or be like the mom who told her daughter the rape was her fault?

That's not what Jesus did.

He rolled up his sleeves and got *involved*.
He listened.
He suffered alongside us.
He came near.

He whispers hope and promises to us in the midst of the pain. It would be helpful if we started to do the same. When I'm struggling, one of the most encouraging things is to just have my friends and family be there for me. Their simple presence—saying nothing, simply sitting there with me—actually says everything. That is a place we need to get to because that is where Jesus is. He intimately involves himself with our grief. He identifies.

As I heard one pastor beautifully say, "The cross is God's way of saying, 'Me too.'"[7]

So continue to tell yourself and others, we need to just be there for each other when in the trenches of suffering. If it is a crazy injustice or evil, continue to reassure the victim that it's not their fault. And if you can't explain it or understand why, don't try to. Be there, be gentle, be vulnerable, be involved, and let God's grace do the talking. Because the truth is, no matter how ugly or how deep the scars, there is always hope. He didn't leave us out in the cold.

## AN ANCHORED HOPE

When it comes to suffering, Christians have the rock-solid hope of resurrection. We have the certified promise that this life is not all there is. There is more. Central to the Christian message is a God who is near, and a God who breathes resurrection into dead things.

There will be a time when God makes it right. First, he will avenge evil. And second, he will restore, redeem, and resurrect everything. So if something evil has happened to you, if you have experienced injustice, never forget that God sees it and is a God of justice. All sin is either paid for by Jesus on the cross or by the person who doesn't trust him at the end of time. As the apostle Paul reminds us, "Never avenge yourselves, but leave it to the wrath of God, for it is written, 'Vengeance is mine, I will repay, says the Lord.'"[8]

That means I can leave the justice to God.

If vengeance is his job and I can trust him to take care of it, then my job is forgiveness.

Too often when I try to avenge my own suffering, I become

bitter toward the other person or the circumstance. The problem with bitterness is that it's like drinking poison, thinking it'll kill the other person—but it kills you instead. But since God has completely forgiven us, we can turn around and forgive as well. God will take care of justice.

The beautiful promise of Jesus is we have the hope of resurrection. The Bible makes it clear that this life isn't the final stage. This is an interim time when sin has been defeated, but we can still feel its effects. Death isn't lord, but it still happens. We are in limbo waiting for that day when heaven and earth are joined together and made new. It's coming.

The writer of Hebrews tells us, "Faith is the assurance of things hoped for, the conviction of things not seen."[9] If you trust in Jesus, you have this hope. He promises you will be made fully alive. All the evil that has been done will be undone. Jesus will come and redeem, renew, and restore. The Bible talks about the final stage as a "new heaven and new earth."[10] It doesn't say babies with wings and harps will be sitting on fluffy clouds. It says God will send a new earth down from heaven.

An actual place without suffering.

Without death.
Without sin.
Without tears.
Without pain.
Without heartache.

That is the place Jesus is bringing, and we have that hope. This life and all its baggage is passing away. We were made for something greater. Something better. Something extraordinary.

In the meantime Jesus has sent his Spirit to comfort us.

To guide us.

To be with us.

To help us grow.

And in the in-between time, he promises he won't leave. Ever.

If you have Jesus, you are not hopeless. People without Jesus don't have this hope. But when you come to him, you have this hope. This life is hard and beats us up, but we have the taste of hope now, and the weight of hope to look forward to:

"Behold, the dwelling place of God is with man. He will dwell with them, and they will be his people, and God himself will be with them as their God. He will wipe away every tear from their eyes, and death shall be no more, neither shall there be mourning, nor crying, nor pain anymore, for the former things have passed away."

And he who was seated on the throne said, "Behold, I am making all things new."[11]

1. Do you view your life—even the difficult parts—as a gift from God? Why or why not?
2. How has God redeemed suffering in your life and made the dark times a blessing?
3. "Beautiful people do not just happen." Do you agree or disagree with this statement? Why or why not?
4. Jeff writes that God gets involved in our mess and our pain because of a deep love for us. How do you respond to that truth?
5. Are there people whom you need to forgive? How can you work toward forgiveness, and maybe reconciliation, in those circumstances to avoid the poison of bitterness?
6. How can you become someone who fully believes in the hope of the resurrection? Would such a belief change your priorities? What other changes might you experience?
7. What is something new that God is making in your life?

# RELIGION SAYS, "GOD WILL LOVE YOU IF . . ." / JESUS SAYS, "GOD SO LOVED . . ."

When I had been following Jesus for almost a year, I was already seen as the token Christian guy on my college baseball team. I didn't go to parties with the team and didn't talk about girls the way they did, so another buddy on the team and I just stuck to ourselves. It was that year when the real, beautiful, and scandalous grace of God knocked me over.

Sure, I had started to follow Jesus.

Sure, I was doing all the "Christian" things.

Sure, I was in forty-seven Bible studies—okay,
  maybe not quite that many.

But God still had a plan to expose the filthiness of my sin completely and blow me up with his grace. When we become Christians, we begin to follow Jesus, but the moments when he completely obliterates our self-righteousness and gives us a potent dose of real, transforming grace is when following him becomes deeply special.

As soon as I started following Jesus, a lot of my temptations completely disappeared, but there was one that didn't seem to want to leave: lust. There were still things I wanted to look at and girls I wanted to talk to. There was something especially potent about this temptation. It would call my name, and I couldn't seem to say no. This would result in an endless cycle of guilt and despair because once I was a Christian, I knew I shouldn't be wanting those things. I was under the false impression that Jesus was supposed to make these temptations disappear instantly. The life I had chosen to live for the previous few years haunted me, chased me, and wooed me all the time.

One night during my sophomore year of college, God decided to show me just how inadequate I was to fight my own sin and just how powerful his grace was to break that sin. I was sitting on the couch in my room playing Halo 3, but quickly became bored. Lustful thoughts started to call my name. I knew I shouldn't give in, but there was still a part of me that thought, *Who cares? What's a little fun? No one will know.*

So I texted a girl I had previously had a completely physical relationship with. She said she wasn't doing anything and wanted to hang out, so I drove over to her house with us both knowing what our intentions were. Even while driving there, I felt this cosmic battle waging in my soul. Part of me deeply wanted it, but another part of me knew there was something better and tried to convince me that sex wouldn't bring the satisfaction it promised. Ultimately, I went through with it. Rather than seeing her as another soul made in the image of God, I saw her as an object. Rather than trusting that God actually wanted to bring me deeper joy, I thought I knew better what would make me happy.

I'll never forget the feeling when I got home. I felt hollow, sick, dirty. I was a Christian now. *I knew better.* I wasn't supposed to do that anymore! On top of that, I felt even more shame because I had planned what I did and had many opportunities to say no. I'd never had this happen before, and I've never had it happen since. The shame and guilt were so palpable that I literally became sick. I stayed up until six o'clock that morning throwing up, feeling so dirty and worthless and thinking I had completely failed God and that he must hate me now.

I thought, *What's more evil? Being blind and living in ignorance, or knowing what is right and still doing what is wrong?* I had known it was wrong, but I did it anyway.

I was just lying there, swimming in my own shame and guilt, when this still, small voice whispered into the depths of my soul:

I *love* you.

I *desire* you.

I *delight* in you.

I saw you were going to do that before I went to the cross, and I still went.

I had a feeling of utter quiet and peace. I didn't hear those words in my ears, but felt them whispered into the depths of my bones. Immediately, relief and the epiphany that I hadn't surprised God rushed over me. I hadn't caught him off guard. When Jesus went to the cross, he saw all I'll ever be, all I'll ever do (including that), and all I'll ever want outside of him; but he joyfully came and got me.[1] He looked down and said, "I want that one."

I couldn't earn it, and I don't deserve it. But he freely loves me and gave me grace. Not only did I not deserve his love in that moment, but if anything, I deserved the opposite. But he chose to let his beauty and splendor pour out of him and into my ugliness.

That's when it hit me: God's grace isn't nice and cute. It's scandalous.

For the first time I realized just how inadequate I was. I realized just how incapable I was of freeing myself from sin. I was sitting in this filth and couldn't get out when grace came and got me. It didn't wait on the outside, but it entered into my struggle. We don't have to hide the fact that we are messy because God doesn't hide the fact that that's exactly the type of people he came to save.

##  SCANDALOUS GRACE

God doesn't hide sin. In fact, he put it on display two thousand years ago in a splintered T-shaped piece of wood. Jesus came down to earth, lived the perfect life we never could have, and died the death we should have. And every drop of blood that poured from him was another drop of love falling on us. Have you ever felt like your sin should be paid for?

It has been.

All our sins.
All our filth.
All our guilt.
All our shame.

Jesus paid the price on our behalf.

That type of grace is dangerous. Looking someone right in the face and saying "forgiven," with no conditions and no contract to sign is dangerous. That type of grace, when understood, turns people's lives upside down. That type of grace allowed twelve ordinary, untrained men to turn the world

135

upside down two thousand years ago. That type of grace allows a martyr to stare into the executioner's face with boldness right before his head is about to be cut off. That is the grace Jesus brought.

For some reason, the only way to spiritual growth is having this truth constantly beaten into our heads. As the old hymn puts it, we are prone to wander and prone to leave the God we love.[2] We can know the truth but not truly understand what that truth means. I particularly like how the apostle Paul says it in Romans: "And to the one who does not work but believes in him who justifies the ungodly, his faith is counted as righteousness."[3]

 Notice that he says that God *justifies the ungodly*. Do you believe in a God who justifies ungodly people? I mean, really? Not the people who have it all together, not the people who are good enough, not the people who try really hard, but the ungodly ones.

> God makes right the ones who aren't right.
> He makes holy the filthy.
> He purifies the impure.
> He calls the wicked blameless.
> He "justifies the ungodly."

It's interesting that when we feel ungodly, we hide, but God doesn't hide in that verse. He boasts that he makes right those who deserve the opposite. In a weird way it seems the only qualification for us to be justified is to actually be *ungodly*. It's like God is saying the only way to qualify is to admit you don't qualify.

And grace comes "to the one who does not work." Now, let me clarify: working isn't a bad thing. Discipline is not a bad thing; in fact, I encourage it. But if we are working to earn salvation, it is a terrible thing. We can't earn God's favor, no matter how hard we try. We will always come up short. When it comes to grace, we don't need to work harder; we need to rest harder. Sometimes the hardest thing to do is stop and rest. In some weird way it takes work to not work for God. Which is why the writer of Hebrews says we need to "strive to enter that rest."[4]

Paul continues, telling the Romans that if Christians don't work and trust in God who justifies the ungodly, then faith is "counted as righteousness." The minute we trust in Jesus, our standing becomes his standing. We no longer represent ourselves; Jesus represents us. Our faith isn't earned. It's counted. When we trust in Jesus, God then looks at us the same way he looks at Jesus. Even when we mess up, God looks at us and says, "Pure, spotless, blameless, perfect, holy, my child, you're free!"

That's what changes a heart and what stirs us to worship. That's what changes someone's life.

You don't have to keep trying.
You don't have to hide your sin.

You just have to trust in Jesus who exchanged
himself for you at the cross.

You just need to surrender: Surrender your sin. Surrender
your guilt. Surrender your life. And surrender yourself as lord.

He took your shame. He took your sin. He took your filth
so that God could be both just and Justifier of those who put
their trust in Jesus. He doesn't just let you off the hook; he
put Jesus on the hook for you. Stop working to do something
Jesus has already done. It is finished. If you trust him, your
faith is counted as righteousness.

## TRUE HEALING

A great example of the clash between religion and grace is
the passage about the adulterous woman in the gospel of
John. It inspired a section in a poem I wrote entitled "Sexual
Healing."[5] Whenever we think we're too dirty or unworthy,
we just have to look at how Jesus interacted with the woman
caught in adultery.[6]

Religious leaders threw her down in the temple and were
ready to execute her. They were hiding behind their laws that
justified stoning her. The story seems to allude that Jesus was
already there teaching the crowd. So when he sees this unfold,
he stops and tells the leaders that any of them who is without
sin is worthy to throw the first stone. Can you imagine the
sound? Silence—and then the echo of stones dropping out

of their hands and footsteps shuffling away. What's interesting is according to Jesus' standard, there was one person who actually had the power to stone her—him. He had the right to stone her—he was without sin—and yet he was the only one in that crowd who didn't want to.

Again Jesus' grace is scandalous. The Pharisees were right: the Law of Moses *did* command they stone that woman.[7] She was guilty and couldn't hide. (Side note: the Law commanded  the man to be stoned too. Where was he? Why wasn't he dragged into the public arena and shamed? Religion always has a double standard.)

I can't imagine the shame that woman had to endure. Being dragged directly from the act of adultery into the public temple courtyard in front of everyone. The vulnerability. The nakedness. In the one moment she could not hide, the voices of religion started to spew out at her: "You're not worthy. You're not good enough. You deserve death."

But then the voice of grace spoke. It thundered through the religious condemnation, and with the authority of God on his lips, whispered, "I don't condemn you. Go and sin no more."

Notice the order. Religion says go and try not to sin anymore, and then I won't condemn you. Jesus reverses it. We understand we are free and no longer condemned and then we can go and live a life of freedom and holiness.

Make this story personal. What are you hiding from God? What, if revealed, would leave you naked and exposed as the adulterous woman was?

Your addiction to power and control?

The pills you take to allay the pain and loneliness?

Deep insecurity?

What if you let his grace touch that area of your life? A lot of times it's not God's grace that is being held back, but rather the fact that we are hiding. We all wear these masks— meaning we all have something we project on the outside to others that doesn't truthfully represent who we are. We hide behind our jobs, behind our accomplishments, behind our athletics, behind our grades, behind our relationships, and so on. We don't want anyone to see who we really are—our true selves.

The problem with wearing masks is even when we receive love, it's really the mask that is receiving the love, not us. Whatever gets thrown at us will always hit the mask and can't penetrate our souls. So it is with God's grace. Every second of every day he pursues us and offers grace, but until we take off our masks, we will never be able to accept it.

When we expose ourselves and are completely vulnerable, we lose control but gain joy and freedom. No matter what your sin is, nothing is outside of grace. No sin is too powerful for God to forgive. Whenever that lie is whispered in my ear, I remember what the apostle Paul said: "Where sin increased, grace abounded all the more."[8]

Grace always wins.

# A TRUE LOVE STORY

Between you and me, I'm a sucker for a good chick flick. I'm not sure I want that fact in print for the world to see, but hey, now that we're friends, I can be honest with you. There is something about a love story that always draws me in.

One of my favorite love stories was written more than twenty-five hundred years ago and can be found in the Old Testament. It's a favorite because it's real—not Disney, not a fairy tale. It involves pain and infidelity, yet grace can be found in the middle of it all. It starts with a man named Hosea, who was chosen by God as a prophet. He was a devout and upright man. If Hosea were around today, I'm sure we'd see him paying his taxes, walking grandmas across the street, and spending his Tuesday and Thursday nights serving at the local homeless shelter.

And then something shocking happens. God tells Hosea to marry a prostitute named Gomer. I love how the Bible puts it: "Go, take to yourself a wife of whoredom and have children of whoredom."[9]

Don't you think that's an odd request from the Creator of the universe? I'm sure a million thoughts were going through Hosea's head. *Really? A prostitute?* I have to believe his pride swelled up: *A prostitute? I deserve better than that. I've been good. Why her, God?*

Nonetheless, he listens and obeys. He pursues and

marries Gomer. He enters into an eternal covenant with a prostitute.

It would make for a good ending if after marrying Hosea, Gomer did a complete 180 and left her job. The problem is, that's not what happened. Unfaithfulness wasn't just an action for Gomer but a lifestyle. Even after being married, she continued to run to those other men. She continued to play the whore. She continued to give herself up. It got so bad that Hosea had to buy back his wife from the slave market.[10] What must have been his range of emotions in that moment: shame, embarrassment, inadequacy?

Can you imagine having to buy your own wife back from the slave market? I'm sure she was standing there in the market-place completely naked. Men cheering, yelling, and holding up coins, bidding on her as if she were a piece of meat. And Hosea standing there with deep anguish, willing to pay the highest price with hope that his wife would just come home.

I'm sure there were moments Hosea railed back against God. *I married her! Isn't that enough?! Do I really have to keep pursuing her? If she doesn't want me, that's her choice!*

It was probably right in that moment that God quietly revealed his purpose. He wasn't having Hosea marry Gomer just to make his life miserable. He told Hosea to marry Gomer in hopes that maybe the nation of Israel would finally see what it was like for God to pursue his people. *We* are the spiritual whores. We give our entire lives on the altar of false gods— money, sex, reputation, work, etc.—and God continues to pursue us. He continues to chase us. He continues to woo us. That is the God of the Bible.

A God of pursuit.

A God of covenant.

A God of unfailing love and grace.

The story as a reflection of us isn't flattering at all. But I love how this story illustrates a powerful reflection of God's true nature. He doesn't just marry us once. He doesn't just come after us once. He doesn't just save us once.[11] When he makes a promise to his people, he keeps it. He doesn't go anywhere, and he is relentless about his pursuit of us. His love isn't soft and fuzzy. It's ferocious, furious, and jealous.[12]

My favorite part of the story is that God doesn't force us to marry him or obey, but like Hosea, he powerfully woos us to him. In the same way Hosea brought Gomer back once and for all, fully restored despite the messy, gritty, unexpected events before, so God in Jesus does the same. We run, we rebel, we turn away, but in Jesus we have an anchor. We have been bought. God's love is so potent that, when it finally pierces the heart, we can't help but have a transformed heart. Too many times people portray God as the ultimate judge, waiting to sentence us for our sins. The truth is, he is a loving husband who compels us with his love and not fear.

Is that the love you know, or do you obey God out of fear? Both fear and love might cause obedience, but only love causes joy. Fear says, "Do this or else you'll be in trouble." The problem with fear-based Christianity is we only obey when the fear is there. If you only want to obey God when you feel threatened by his commands, it's not God you worship, but your fear.

Love, however, compels a heart and produces lasting joy and obedience. Hosea's love was so powerful, so relentless, it slowly but surely drew Gomer back into the covenant. Never once did he threaten her with divorce, but instead he just showered more grace.

God's grace is so much more powerful of a motivator than fear. Love is the deepest motivator. Only love can produce not only willing obedience but also *lasting* obedience. If you are being motivated by fear, rules, anger, or some other emotion, it usually only lasts while that emotion is there. Love, being a state of the heart, lasts even past the initial emotion.

## WE AREN'T GOD'S EMPLOYEES

In the story of Hosea and Gomer we see that God is a God of covenant. Covenant love is a love that implies deep commitment and promise. It's not based on feelings or on the other person's actions but on the initiating person's good pleasure. God loves because he *is* love. He doesn't love because we are lovable. There is a difference.

The idea of covenant has long been seen in many of our most precious relationships. Sadly, some of them have been completely eroded. Consider the marriage relationship. Because of selfishness we no longer promise to be with someone until we die. We might say, "Until death do us part," but we really mean, "Until you stop satisfying or fulfilling me." Of course we'd never admit it, but the divorce rates say enough. Divorce has become normal. Rather than love being an action of self-will and commitment, we've turned it into a shallow emotion whose absence warrants separation.

We don't treat the parent-child relationship like that, though. Imagine a kid spilling something on the floor and the parent saying, "Forget it! I'm out of here. I guess I just don't love you anymore." We immediately know that's not okay. We still believe the parental relationship is like a covenant that cannot be broken. We should view the marriage relationship the same. God uniquely highlights marriage as one of the main ways we know who he is and how he relates to us. That's why Jesus is so strongly against divorce. Every time divorce occurs, the couple is telling a lie about God's relationship with humanity. He never leaves because we are under covenant.

One of the most blatant places God shows us the importance of covenant is in the story of the prodigal son, which I've already partially shared in chapter 3. Something really interesting takes place right in the middle of the story.

The younger son had just completely wrecked his life. He took all his inheritance and spent every last dime. He had nothing to show for it except empty pockets and an empty heart. While eating with the pigs, he came to himself and realized that back home even his father's servants were living better than he was. So he said to himself, "I will arise and go to my father, and I will say to him, 'Father, I have sinned against heaven and before you. I am no longer worthy to be called your son. Treat me as one of your hired servants.'"[13]

I find it interesting that the son practices his coming-home speech before he actually comes home. He's not the only one! I do that all the time. When I mess up, I quickly think of the best apology I can give to God or anyone else before I actually approach them.

But as the son came home, the father spotted him from a distance. He then ran to his son, embraced him, hugged him, and kissed him. Notice that the father ran. He was the one doing the pursuit. He didn't wait for the son to come groveling home. On top of that, in the Hebrew culture, it was shameful for an old man to run—and if you have seen some dads run, you know this should be an American tradition too. Yet the father didn't care. He ran. He faced the embarrassment. He took the reproach. Then he embraced his son.

Where had the son come from? It says he came from the pigpen, which means he probably had mud and feces all over him. And when you hug someone who is filthy, you get filthy.

That's a picture of Jesus on the cross, with his arms stretched wide, absorbing and soaking in all our filth. He doesn't wait for us to clean up. He simply hugs us and gets all our dirt on himself.

So as they hug, the son gives his dad the speech he

practiced earlier: "Father, I have sinned against heaven and before you. I am no longer worthy to be called your son."[14]

I always imagine the father saying, "Yes, you have been bad. Yes, you are no longer worthy to be called a son. You must work around the house to make up for it and pay me back." But that's not even close to what he really says. In fact, what he says might even be considered rude! He doesn't even acknowledge the son's repentance speech.

> But the father said to his servants, "Bring quickly the best robe, and put it on him, and put a ring on his hand, and shoes on his feet. And bring the fattened calf and kill it, and let us eat and celebrate. For this my son was dead, and is alive again; he was lost, and is found." And they began to celebrate.[15]

In other words, "Stop groveling. You're home. That's all that matters. Let's party."

Even though the son asked to be treated like an employee or servant of the father, the father refused. "You're my son." He didn't give him an opportunity to pay him back but instead gave him full rights as his child. The ring and the robe signified full restitution with the family.

Don't we do that with God all the time?

We'd rather be his employees than his children.
We'd rather be under contract than under covenant.

We so desperately want to earn it. To pay it back. To merit something good in ourselves.

But the scandalous part about grace is, we don't work for God. He actually works for us. How outrageous is that? He  brings us into the family, not into the company. When it sinks in that once we trust in Jesus we are eternally his, we immediately feel security and freedom.

There is no security in being an employee. The contract can be breached. When you are an employee and something goes wrong, you can get fired. But when you are a child who is having a season of struggle or waywardness, parents become more intimately involved in your life! That's true with every parent I see. When the kid is struggling, when the kid is rebelling, parents don't "fire" the kid. They actually stay up even later thinking, praying, and pursuing that child. The child actually gets *more* attention.

So it is with God and us. He doesn't leave us. And when we are messing up or struggling, he actually gives us even more attention. There is no earning when it comes to being a child. You simply *are*.

My dad's name is Gary Bethke. Imagine if someone came up to me and asked me, "Jeff, are you Gary Bethke's son?" How weird would it sound if I said, "Well, you know, I really want to be, and I'm trying to be, but it's hard." I can only imagine the look that person would give me. You don't *try* to be someone's child. You just are. So why do we do that when someone asks us, "Are you a Christian?" It doesn't make sense to say, "Well, I'm trying."

You don't have to try to be God's daughter or son. You just are. He has become both our eternal Father and our eternal Husband. He uses the most permanent relationships we can comprehend on earth to describe his relationship with us.

## TRUE FREEDOM

One of my favorite things about the grace of God is that rarely in Scripture do you see it demand some sort of action as a payback. Grace just flows. It's a one-way type of love that runs the conduit directly from God's heart to ours.

That kind of grace is scandalous.

A lot of religiously minded people love to say things such as, "You better watch out, grace that free will produce a ton of hypocrites who take advantage of it. Everyone will be saying, 'Well, I can just be forgiven.'"

"Pure anarchy," they say.

The truth is, yes, you can take advantage of it. That's what makes it grace. The receiving party has the opportunity to be hurt. Grace is extremely vulnerable. But in that vulnerability you find people being completely transformed by grace's power and never wanting to take advantage of it. When you hear that you are free, there is nothing sweeter than giving up your entire life for the one who set you free.

Only people who see God as their judge, not their father, try to take advantage of grace. People all the time ask themselves, "How close can I get to this line without getting in trouble?" when it comes to a lawful or judicial relationship, but rarely does someone ask that question when it comes to an intimate relationship. How stupid would I look if I asked, "How close can I get to not loving Alyssa without her divorcing me?" No, I ask how close can I get *to* Alyssa. I'm pursuing her, not running *from* her.

There is an old tale about Abraham Lincoln buying back a slave from the marketplace. He bought the woman and then left. He simply saw her in her slavery and wanted to set her free. She quickly followed and asked, "Sir, you bought me. What do you want from me?"

He responded, "You are free. I just wanted to let you out of bondage. You are free to do whatever you'd like now. That's the definition of free."

She didn't believe it. "Free? Free to do whatever I want?"

He said yes.

"Free to be whatever I want?"

He said yes.

"Free to go wherever I want?"

He said yes again.

She then said with a smile on her face, "If that's the case and I am truly free to do whatever I want, then I'm following you."[16]

When you understand how great the gift you have been given by Jesus is, you can't help but follow him. Since he gave up his life for you, you can't help but give yours back to him.

That is the scandal of grace. I fully believe that as a Christian you can take advantage of grace, but when you've truly tasted it, you never will. When you've experienced the joy and life of Christ in you, then nothing is as satisfying anymore. It's not that you want to use his grace to do all the things you used to love. Those things no longer are attractive to you, and you love *him* now!

There is something about that grace, though, that just rubs some religious people the wrong way. It used to rub me the same way too. True grace can't be controlled. It can't be tamed. It can't be used by the leadership as a social construc tion to manipulate the people. It's wild. And you have to trust it will do its job.

In Greek mythology, the Sirens were extremely seductive characters. They were mermaid-like females who lived on an island and would lure passing boats with their entrancing music and singing. Innocent sailors would follow their voices to the shallowest parts of the sea where they would be ship- wrecked. It was believed that sailors learned where the Sirens were, and so they would do everything possible to block the Sirens' songs.

In Homer's epic poem *The Odyssey*, the sailors stuffed wax into their ears to keep from being seduced to their deaths.

In order for Odysseus to hear the music—and presumably to know when it was safe for the others to unblock their ears— he demanded his men tie him to the mast so he was unable to steer the boat. While they pass near the Sirens, Odysseus demands to be set free so he can go to them, but his men only tie him tighter to the mast.[17]

In Apollonius's epic poem *Argonautica*, which tells the story of Jason stealing the golden fleece, the story of the Sirens is told with a different detail. The island of Sirens is present and a boat is approaching just as before. In this version, how- ever, the Sirens are human-bird hybrids, and the sailors don't use wax to stuff in their ears. The Argonauts are saved from the Sirens by a man named Orpheus. Orpheus, instead of tying men up or stuffing wax in their ears, starts playing his lyre to drown out the Sirens once he sees his men moving to dive into the water. He did exactly what the Sirens did, except his music was louder and more attractive. Because of this all the men were saved except one. They didn't have to tie them- selves up and force themselves not to go anywhere because their ears were "filled with sound of his twanging; and the lyre overcame the maidens' voice."[18]

That's the truth with God's grace. It's not that we are holding on tight in hopes of not being seduced by our old lives and sin, but rather it's that God's grace is so sweet and precious it compels us to stay with it. Grace is better music than sin. We don't want to take advantage of it because there is nothing better out there to take advantage of it for. In the same way that Orpheus's music was beautiful, so God's grace is an alluring, compelling, stunning, and powerful force that invites us to get lost in it.

We don't say, "Oh, I better not do that or God will get me."

Instead we say, "His grace is so much better than whatever anything else is offering."

We don't please God when we white-knuckle or "tie ourselves up" to our obedience. We please him by showing the world just how enjoyable he *really* is.

The best part about that type of grace is that it changes people. Real grace loves us right where we are, but it loves us too much to keep us there. Cheap grace—which is not really grace at all—is like a horrendous version of love that sees its loved one in danger and simply says, "I love you." That doesn't cut it. We need *rescuing*. And God does exactly that. We know we've accepted God's transforming grace if we begin to look different. Don't think grace is beyond your grasp. God is offering it to you.

It's free.

And it's life-giving.

Will you trust him?

1. Jeff writes that Jesus knows all about his sins, and yet when he went to the cross he said, "I want that one." How do you respond to Jesus' powerful love for you?
2. Is your understanding of grace scandalous? Explain.
3. What masks do you wear? How do they keep you from God's grace?
4. Through the prophet Hosea, we learn that God chases us with wild abandon. Have you ever felt wooed by God? If so, describe what it was like.
5. Do you view your relationship with God more as a covenant or a contract? Why?
6. God's grace is described in this chapter as being better than anything else the world has to offer. Think of someone you know who really needs that grace. How might you describe it to them?

# CHAPTER 9

# RELIGION POINTS TO A DIM FUTURE / JESUS POINTS TO A BRIGHT FUTURE

When I first became a Christian, I thought that only religious things mattered, like Bible study, prayer, worship songs, and Sundays. I thought that I was simply supposed to hold on tightly until I got to the finish line. When I finally reached the end, I was sure everything would blow up, and we'd live happily ever after in the white, fluffy clouds of heaven.

That was until I read Romans 8:

For the creation was subjected to futility, not willingly, but because of him who subjected it, in hope that the creation itself will be set free from its bondage to corruption and obtain the freedom of the glory of the children of God. For we know that the whole creation has been groaning together in the pains of childbirth until now.[1]

Even the creation feels the bondage and corruption of sin, is groaning in pain, and will somehow "be set free from its bondage" the same time we are. At first you might think that sounds a little hippie-like. The verse almost seems that God has made a covenant with his creation just as he has with us.

That's when it hit me: God actually cares about a lot of things we don't.

> God actually cares about the earth, but we seem to
> think it's going to burn.
> God actually cares about creating good art, but we
> seem to think it's reserved for salvation messages.
> God actually cares about mundane jobs, when we
> seem to think only "Christian ministry" will make
> him happy.

Our lives on earth aren't just placeholders until we go to heaven. We are to create, cultivate, and redeem while we're here. The misconception, I've realized, has come from a lack of knowledge of why we were created.

# WHAT WE WERE CREATED
## *AS* AND CREATED *FOR*

To understand why we were created, we need to go back to the ancient garden. The one where everyone walked around naked, there was no sin, and animals such as gorillas and lions probably roamed freely next to Adam and Eve. Pretty epic time in history, if you ask me. As the book of Genesis records, "God said, 'Let us make man in our image, after our likeness. And let them have dominion over the fish of the sea and over the birds of the heavens and over the livestock and over all the earth and over every creeping thing that creeps on the earth.'"[2]

God, when he created humankind, created us in his image. God had created everything up to that point, but he hadn't created anything "in his image." In the Old Testament, the phrase "image of God" is only found three times, all in Genesis referring to God creating humans. We are the only ones created in his image, which means we bear some form of God's nature and reflection in us and on us.

The fact that we can create is a sign we are created in his image. No other creatures have this ability to create. Sure, some animals can build and work, but they can't *create*. They can't make something out of nothing. I've yet to see a horse write a screenplay for an award-winning movie or a shark paint a sunset on canvas. Only humans are uniquely wired to create.

As God's children, we are to use our lives knowing they

reflect back to him and bear his image. Too often, instead of acting like mirrors pointing back to Jesus, we try to act like billboards, advertising ourselves. But outside of Jesus we have no ability to create. In the same way the moon can't light up without the sun—because all it is doing is reflecting the sunlight—we can't create or bear God's image on our own accord. Trying to get glory for things we have done is like the moon shouting, "Look how awesome I am," when the only reason the moon is shining in the first place is because of the sun. The brightness of the moon is *borrowed* brightness.

This is partially why God wants us to be involved in his creation, managing it and cultivating it. For example, Alyssa is a photographer, and I doubt it would go well for me if I said, "Hey, Alyssa, I really love you, but I hate your photography. It's pointless and seems like a waste of time." I can guarantee she'd be pretty mad at me. Photography is something she does, and it has her image on it. When I praise her photography, I'm praising *her.*

I show her I love her by also loving what she creates. So it is with God. We can't say we love him if we don't also love what he has created. This applies to people of different races, cultures, and countries. Since everyone is made in the image of God, everyone has worth and everyone has dignity. You want to radically change how you see others? See them as fellow image bearers—broken just like you, but image bearers nonetheless.

We love God by loving his people.

## CHRISTIAN MINISTRY

When I first became a Christian, I had a ton of passion but no knowledge. Even when I had been a Christian for a total of four seconds, I thought I knew exactly what God wanted and desired regarding a ton of different issues. For example, alcohol was a sin. There was no arguing that one. I even refused to read Jesus' first miracle for what it was.

Drunkenness? Yes, that's a sin.

Making a brother or sister stumble? Yes, definitely a sin.

But alcohol as sinful in and of itself? Still can't find a verse. Same with tattoos.

But the big one I'd harp on to all my friends was secular music. There was no way you could be a Christian if you listened to music that was made by the devil's puppets. If the song didn't say things like "amen," "hallelujah," and "transubstantiation"—even though I didn't know what that last term meant—it was not okay in my mind. Because of this I did something I regret to this day.

At the time, I had an enormous iTunes library, and maybe only 20 percent of it was labeled "Christian," so I devoted a whole night to scrolling through my entire list of music, highlighting, right clicking, and pressing *move to trash*. I probably put thousands of songs in the trash can. And then for the big crescendo, I right clicked and pressed *empty trash can*. I'll be honest: in that moment, I felt pretty holy. I felt God smiling down on me. I mean, how could he not let me into heaven after deleting Lil' Wayne from my iPod playlist, right?

Then about a year or two later, after almost constant Bible study, I started to ask those questions that just gnaw at you. Why was there such a thing as "Christian music" anyway? Music can't be saved. When I bought those songs, it wasn't like I baptized them and gave them communion before I listened to them. I wanted to know what actually made music Christian. And why was Christianity the only religion that had our music separated by faith rather than genre?

How come when I go to the music store, I don't see a Muslim section, an atheist section, and an agnostic section? Doesn't that seem weird that all music is separated by genre except Christian music, which is separated by worldview? That's an indictment on both the Christian and the non-Christian: on the Christian because we like to retreat to our own subculture, and on the non-Christian because they don't let Jesus followers have a voice in the industry at-large.

I started to miss some of the music I had deleted. I thought Christian music would grow on me, but it never seemed to. A lot of times it felt outdated, cheesy, and generic. The lyrics were fine, but some of the music was terrible. FYI, if you can replace God's name with your girlfriend's name in the song, it's probably not all that deep or theologically dense.

The more I pushed into the Scriptures, the more I

realized Christians hadn't gotten this view from the Bible. The idea originated with Greek philosophers who pushed a heavy secular-versus-sacred agenda. They said there were things of the body that were mundane and things of the spirit that were important. But God never stated this. Genesis 1 says everything he created was good.

*Everything.*

That means music, art, politics, food, animals, plants, and trees are all good in and of themselves.

These things aren't evil, but our abuse of them is evil. You'd be hard-pressed to find something that the Bible calls inherently evil. Almost everything the Bible condemns is an abuse of God's original intent or use when he created it. God created everything, so it doesn't have to be labeled "Christian" to be good. He created the trees. He created molecules. He created taste buds that send amazing signals to my brain every time I have Alyssa's homemade guacamole. How could I not give him glory for that? There is no divide between secular and sacred, and we completely miss it when we insist there is.

As Christians we should be setting the bar for good art and culture, not trying to sequester ourselves away and only copying other art in order to make it "Christian." After all, we have the Creator as our Dad, and if we suck at creating, then we're sinning. Now, that might seem a little harsh, but it should inspire us to shoot for more. We need to see the gravity of our actions. As image bearers, we are to reflect a proper image of who God is. When we make bad things, we are reflecting a false image of who God is.

> We are saying God is a copycat, when he isn't.
> We are saying God is cheesy, when he isn't.
> We are saying God doesn't believe in the excellence
>   of all things, when he does.
> We are lying.

Growing up I only saw art in the church when it was a portrayal of Jesus' blood or a graphic picture of the cross. I remember thinking, *Is there no such thing as art in the Christian world outside of salvation? Can art just speak for itself as something beautiful and true and point to Jesus?* A depiction of his sacrifice on our behalf is amazing, but let's also display beauty and wonder in the everyday as awesome too.

At the end of his life, the apostle Paul was talking to his protégé Timothy and wrote, "For everything created by God is good, and nothing is to be rejected if it is received with thanksgiving, for it is made holy by the word of God and prayer."[3] God should get a lot more glory for things than we give him.

If we only give God glory for explicitly Christian things, we are thieves. He wants all the glory. When we bite into food, we are to let him know how awesome he is for making food. When we listen to great music, we are to do the same. When we don't, we are stealing. There is glory God deserves that he is not being given.

I struggled with this a ton in college. I'd spend time praying in the morning and then proceed to class. But sometimes I'd have tough thoughts, or feel like what I was doing had no benefit. I just wanted to get back to my room to pray and read my Bible. Now, those things are great, but I missed God in everyday life when he was there the whole time. He was in my classroom just as much as he was in my bedroom. He was present, wanting glory for the meal I ate that day just as much as he wanted glory when praying to him.

I took this line of thinking all the way into my vocation. I quit baseball my senior year of college because I wanted to concentrate on studying the Scriptures and pursuing a more "righteous" job like being a pastor or theologian. Now, studying the Scriptures is vital to a healthy life with Jesus, and technically, we are all theologians. Some of us just have terrible theology. But I thought I needed to get a Christian job. To this day I wonder, *Who showed Jesus to the other players once I left the team?* God had given me the unique ability of baseball to infiltrate that culture as a missionary, knowing the language and customs to point people to Jesus.

When I first became a Christian, I thought that to be a good Christian, I had to be in ministry. I thought people who weren't were just Junior Varsity Christians. I thought that to be on God's good side, you needed to be a pastor, theologian, or priest. You could maybe be a Bible study leader, but that was pushing it. It was almost not holy enough. Being a Bible study leader was like being on the swing team in high school sports—where you'd play on JV but sometimes get the privilege of sitting on the varsity bench. But that's not what the Bible says.

Peter was a fisherman.

Paul was a tent maker.

Jesus was a carpenter.

Does that strike anyone as weird? Jesus literally made things out of wood all day. He wasn't a temple priest; he was a carpenter. An average blue-collar, nine-to-five workingman. Scares me to think how quickly I would pass him today if I saw him on the street. Probably would be a construction worker with calloused hands, wearing a Carhartt jacket.

In fact, few people switched vocations after they began to follow Jesus the first two hundred years of Christianity, unless their vocations outright violated Scripture, as prostitution and sorcery do. Since Christians were persecuted, they worked as they always had to provide for their families, and then maybe they led or pursued other ministries in the underground church. But for the most part if a blacksmith became a Christian, he stayed a blacksmith. He was just a blacksmith to the glory of God.

As the apostle Paul made it clear, "So, whether you eat or drink, or whatever you do, do all to the glory of God."[4] There's no asterisk after that verse that adds, "Only if that eating or drinking is done in an overtly Christian way like at communion or a church potluck." No, it says whatever you do. No qualifications. No exceptions. Now, if the Bible calls it a sin, or if you know you are blatantly doing it to the glory of yourself rather than God, then don't do it. But we have to admit we don't give God the glory he deserves.

You can bring God glory wherever he has already placed you. You don't need to feel guilty that you're a chef. You don't need to feel guilty that you only paint, but your dad wants you to be a pastor. Too many times Christians want to go into ministry because of outside pressures by their parents or pastors, not realizing where they already are is their mission field.

Single moms, I'm going to come right out and say it: don't struggle under the burden of wanting to do more outside your home but not being able to, especially if you have small children. You don't need to lead a women's group, write a Bible study, or serve in your neighborhood. Your kids take up all your time, as they should at this stage in your life. You don't need to be leading a ministry. Your kids are your ministry!

The apostle Paul tasks Christians with a "ministry of reconciliation,"[5] which sounds pretty opened-ended to me. You can worship God by cleaning up baby puke with a thankful heart just as much as if you were to be writing a Bible study for thousands of people. This is because the way you train that child, the way you teach him the ways of Jesus, and the way you display grace and truth firsthand is God displaying his ministry of reconciliation through you. God is pleased with you. It comes down to a thankful heart, not an explicitly

Christian behavior. If something is done with a thankful heart, then that is Christian behavior.

Christianity will spread quickly when there are disciples of Jesus living in every domain of society—service, politics, music, art, etc.—bringing glory to him and pursuing the greatest joy possible.

> Do you like to cook? Do it to the glory of God.
> Do you like to work on cars? Do it to the glory of
>   God.
> Do you like to write stories? Do it to the glory of God.

If you have a thankful heart and are using that domain to reflect God's beauty as Creator, then you are worshiping. Listening to Hillsong United isn't worship; it's an aid for worship. I found a deeper level of joy and connection with Jesus when I realized that eating a good meal with thankfulness was just as holy as my prayer time. The truth is, God doesn't just want your "Christian" things. He wants it all. When we realize the beauty of God's grace in the mundane, not just the religious, that's when we will begin to see him correctly.

## TRUE WORSHIP

In the New Testament, Jesus encounters a promiscuous Samaritan woman. I've mentioned parts of this story in chapter 4, but to recap, since Jesus was a Jew, he shouldn't have been talking to her. Samaritans were seen by Jews as half-breed, marginalized people. To make matters worse, she was a woman, a second-class citizen during this time, and a promiscuous one at that! Thank goodness Jesus wasn't running for president, as his association with her would have been a PR nightmare. He didn't seem to care too much about the societal rules and standards—what else is new—and so he engaged her in conversation. With a bit of humor, Jesus asked her to go get her husband. When she told him she didn't have one, Jesus pretty much said, "I know the guy you are messing around with now isn't your husband."

The woman said to him, "Sir, I perceive that you are a prophet. Our fathers worshiped on this mountain, but you say that in Jerusalem is the place where people ought to worship." Jesus said to her, "Woman, believe me, the hour is coming when neither on this mountain nor in Jerusalem will you worship the Father. You worship what you do not know; we worship what we know, for salvation is from the Jews. But the hour is coming, and is now here, when the true worshipers will worship the Father in spirit and truth, for the Father is seeking such people to worship him. God is spirit, and those who worship him must worship in spirit and truth."[6]

The Jews and the Samaritans argued about the right place to worship. Was it just in Jerusalem, or were their old places just as good? But Jesus says to forget that. He says upon his death and resurrection things are going to change radically. No longer will worship be an external behavior with certain holy spots, but holiness will be a matter of worshiping in spirit and in truth. Faith is no longer wrapped up in a building; it's wrapped up in every soul who loves Jesus. When the people of God move, the church moves. It's not brick and mortar; it's skin and bone.

The best part about this Bible passage is it tells us what God is seeking. We don't have to guess—we don't have to blindly attempt to please him—because he tells us. He is seeking worshipers who worship in spirit and in truth.

The word *worship* is defined by glory and thanksgiving. We are worshiping when we give glory to something. Whatever we give glory to, we sacrifice for. Sometimes that's sex; sometimes that's our jobs; sometimes that's our reputations. But we all worship something, and we all put pseudo-gods on the thrones of our hearts.

When Jesus died on the cross, he completely reversed this curse, allowing God to retake his proper place as the one true God of our lives.

Proper worship is living a life in spirit *and* truth.

God owns every bit of truth in this entire universe. If something is true, it's his. He is the source of all truth and light, so if something is true, it is coming from him. This means he can get worship from something if it's true.

Take Michael Jackson's song "Man in the Mirror." I love

that song, but I've had many Christians say that it's not okay to listen to it. The artist wasn't a Christian, so God can't get glory from it.

I see it differently.

The reason I like that song is because it's *true*. The entire premise is that to make a change in the world, you need to start with yourself and look in the mirror. That is true, correct? And so when I hear that song, it is worship to me because it stirs my affections toward Jesus, makes me realize I need to concentrate on my sin more than anyone else's sin, and encourages me to go out and make a difference.

We should not consolidate God's glory to only explicitly "Christian" things. We owe God more praise than we think. On top of that, how big and great is a God who can get glory and praise out of a song written by someone who doesn't love him? He's that big. God gets glory for everything, and everyone eventually will glorify God, be it his grace or his justice.

Let's take classical music as another example. There aren't usually lyrics, but there is an extremely beautiful collision of instruments and sounds. When I hear that music, I listen to how amazing the different instruments are, and it stirs thankfulness in my heart toward God. How awesome is he that he created the instruments to sound like they do? How awesome is he that he created our ears to receive the sounds so poetically? The minute my heart and mind give him praise for that, it's worship.

In the book of Acts, the apostle Paul uses a pagan philosopher to prove his point. Truth is truth no matter if it comes out of the mouth of a donkey, a philosopher, or the apostle himself.[7] In fact, if we are honest, a lot of times when we reject truth coming from a non-Christian source, we are trying to justify disobedience.

For those who might be unsure about this issue, let me ask: Why don't we do it with anything else? Why don't we do it with doctors? How awkward would it be if we asked our surgeon just before being rolled into the operating room, "Are you a Christian? If not, you can't perform surgery on me!" That would be insane. We judge doctors based on their field and expertise. Either the doctor is good at medicine or he or she isn't. And you can give God glory and praise when you walk out of the operating room a healed person because he has uniquely given that doctor a gift in order to bring God praise, whether the doctor is a Christian or not.

So it is with art and music. It's not about a piece being Christian; it's about a piece being true, beautiful, and excellent. As the apostle Paul tells us, "For from him and through him and to him are all things. To him be glory forever."[8]

God is glorified in everything he has created. Am I saying everything needs to be received with open arms? Not at all! There are plenty of things people in the world say that are not true in the biblical sense. That's why we have to be in the Scriptures. Scripture is our litmus test. Does it line up? Does it hold up? Is it according and similar to God's character revealed in Jesus? Have a filter, and make sure it is truth according to God.

Jesus made the elements of worship extremely clear: spirit *and* truth. For something to be considered proper worship, it's got to be both. The problem is some of us are very good at worshiping in spirit but not in truth, while others are good at worshiping in truth but not in spirit.

The ones who worship in spirit and not in truth are easy to spot. They usually say things like, "I'm spiritual but not religious." They usually base their lives on the five senses. If it feels good, tastes good, or smells good, it must be right. They are caught up in the whims of their emotions and lusts.

They are the same type of people the apostle Paul addressed in Athens. He walked into the town and saw the idols everywhere, and it grieved him.[9] There was a ton of worship going on, just not *right* worship. That's when he exposed the futility of their idols. He made it very clear the gods of sex, money, and power couldn't save. They were made with human hands and could do nothing for them. Think about it: When was the last time your boyfriend set you free from all that enslaves you? What else or who else died so that you could be made new? Idols always overpromise and underdeliver.

The opposite distortion is also easy to see. Someone who worships in truth but not in spirit usually has nineteen Bibles on their shelves—all with dust on them. They can tell you the Ten Commandments even though they hardly live by them. They seem to know rules but lack gentleness, love, and compassion. They seem rigid. There is no wiggle room. They worship by the letter of the law, not the spirit of the law as the Bible says.[10]

But combining worship with spirit and truth is a beautiful thing. Truth with the Spirit becomes vibrant, organic, and alive. It feels fresh and new. Thankfulness sparks in a heart frequently. That's true worship.

## THE BIGGEST LIE

God cares about every domain of life—politics, science, food, art, and music are all his, which means he wants them all back. He wants the glory. He wants redemption in those fields. And he redeemed us that we might turn around and continue his redemptive work in all these other areas. We are created to cultivate, not just talk about religious things all day. Jesus makes it very clear that he came to build his kingdom. That implies not just a group of people but a way of life fully encompassing all matter and substance.

He came not to save people but to save his entire creation, which we are a part of. It's about restoration. If we don't realize this, we will naturally turn to escapism rather than restoration. We will turn church into a holy huddle rather than a group of people sent out to push back the domain of darkness. We are created to infect and infiltrate culture, restoring and reclaiming what is God's.

Music? That's God's.

Sex? That's his too.

Art? He is the ultimate creator, after all.

We are to show a different way of life right in the middle of culture rather than creating our own subculture.

The problem with the American-Christian subculture is that our art and glorification of Jesus begin to weaken because we lose all sense of comparison. For example, a lot of Christian musicians no longer shoot to be the best musicians; they shoot to be the best Christian musicians. The standards have been lowered. But the truth is, art can speak for itself. It is a reflection of the creation mandate, not the salvation mandate. Rather than making Christian music, we should make music with a Christian worldview just as atheists, Muslims, and others do when they make music. There is nothing about music that is Christian; it's the worldview in the music that can be.

When we privatize our art to the Christian sector, we see churches feeling the need to be relevant rather than just using their gifts to reflect who God is and what he is like. The problem with trying to be relevant is it makes us copy what culture is already doing. To be relevant, you have to copy what is cool. So we put our mouths on the tailpipe of secular culture in hopes we can recycle some of it and use it for ourselves.

The problem with this is that it automatically puts us ten to fifteen years behind culture because rather than setting the precedent, we are copying their systems. This is where we get a huge section of Christian apparel and coffee mugs that simply copy secular logos. My favorite is the shirt with the words "Holy Spirit" printed in the same font and logo as Sprite. Or the one with "A bread crumb and a fish" instead of Abercrombie and Fitch.

We call it redeeming, but it's actually stealing.

Making bad art is bad in and of itself, but if we are Christians, this takes on a whole other level of weight. Because we are called to mirror and reflect God, everything we do should give people a proper picture of who he is. Our job as Christians is to stick so close to Jesus that when people are around us, they sense him. Is that true with your life? With your job? With your hobbies?

The problem with bad art and creating a Christian subculture is it tells a lie about God. When we become lazy and only copy other art in order to make it Christian, we are sinning. We are saying God is a copycat and that he needs culture's creativity. If God is the Creator, though, shouldn't the people who are in relationship with him be the most creative? So when we make art and when we engage the culture, what kind of picture and message are we giving about God?

The truth is, God is a God of excellence. He does things well. He goes above and beyond. He lavishes excessively and adds nuances simply to bring his name glory. Does the way we do art, the way we engage politics, and the way we eat food give this image of God? Too many times we retreat, when God wants us to engage.

When Jesus is speaking to Peter about starting the church, Jesus says, "The gates of hell shall not prevail against it."[11] The crazy thing about that statement is gates don't move on their own. For them to "not prevail," something has to be charging them because they are a defensive structure. Jesus is implying that the church will be storming the gates of hell, not running the opposite way. We should be engaging and pushing back the realms of darkness as a powerful offensive force. He doesn't say we should retreat, escape, and hold on tightly because the powers of hell are chasing us in the domain of secular music and evil movies. No, he is saying to infiltrate and infect every domain in life with his grace.

There is no divide between secular and sacred, and we completely miss worship when we insist on it. God created everything, so something doesn't have to be explicitly Christian. We should judge things based on beauty and truth. God owns truth and has a monopoly on truth. As Christians, we should be setting the bar for good art and culture.

## BUILDING THE CITY

After realizing I no longer had to attend seminary in order to be a good Christian, I felt free. Truth is, I wasn't any good at learning Greek or Hebrew, and I certainly wouldn't have enjoyed it. But what could I do? I love to write, speak, blog, and make creative YouTube videos with my friends. I began to see the creative process as a form of worship to my Creator.

What does this look like for you? We are all called to be ambassadors and missionaries for Christ.[12] Missionaries, by definition, engage in the culture around them and show people Jesus and his grace in that particular context. What do you truly love to do? Are you an artist? Do you love to cook? Do you enjoy dancing?

The psalmist says, "Delight yourself in the LORD, / and he will give you the desires of your heart."[13] I find it scandalous that God will give us our desires.

Augustine wrote, "Love, and do what you will," in reference to 1 John 4:8.[14] I remember thinking, *Do as I will? That sounds dangerous.* The truth is, when we are living for God, our desires are actually God's desires. The question shouldn't be, am I in God's will? The harder question for me is, am I actually delighting myself in the Lord? Because if you can answer yes to the second, then you can answer yes to the first. John MacArthur, a famous Bible teacher, gave us a few questions to ask ourselves:

1. Are you saved?
2. Are you spirit-filled? *Are you living moment by moment in his presence?*
3. Are you sanctified? *Are you set apart to him?*
4. Are you submissive? *Are you holding everything with an open hand?*
5. Are you thankful?

God makes it pretty clear that if you can answer yes to all these questions, you can do whatever you want.[15] Why? Because if those things are true, God will give you the desires of your heart, which are intertwined with his. You don't need a spooky ghost to show up and tell you what to do. You don't need to burn some incense and light some candles. You can live in the freedom that if you are living close to Jesus, you can do as you please. If one of your answers is no, then your desires may not be lining up with God's, so you have to be careful.

So what drives you? What do you like to do? Do it and thank God while you're in the middle of doing it. That's true worship. And when we're all following our desires, every part of culture is being influenced. God calls us to create and cultivate every domain.

Genesis starts in a garden, but Revelation ends in a city. I find that so interesting since you can't get from a garden to a city without cultivating and creating. We have to get there somehow. We were not called to retreat into the forest, read Left Behind books, and play harps until we get to heaven. We are called to redeem this earth—everything, not just the spiritual part. Jesus is Lord of all of it, even the mundane Mondays through Saturdays. He's not just in charge of Sundays.

Have you ever stared at a downtown skyline and been in awe? I've been to Manhattan a few times, and the buildings and infrastructure are incredible. Every time I walk by the Empire State Building, down Wall Street, or through Times

Square, all I can think is, *If this is what broken and fallen men and women can make, what will be in store for us who love Jesus and are in glory with him? If we can create this in our broken vessels, what will we be able to create when fully restored?*

We need to start seeing ourselves as missionaries and ambassadors for Christ in everything. Where does God want to send you as a missionary for culture? One of my favorite examples is Lecrae. Most people my age know his music. He's a beast hip-hop artist, but he sees everything about his craft—the songs, the interviews, the content—intentionally. He sees himself as an urban missionary in a particular context and desires that people with a Christian worldview have a seat at the mainstream table. He does everything with that lens. He doesn't do this so he can get famous. He does it so he can make disciples.

When there's a shooting in Chicago and the news wants a hip-hop perspective, he wants the reporters to call him. When there is a segment on mistreatment of women in hip-hop, he wants to be interviewed. He does this so he can articulate the good news of Jesus in mediums that might not otherwise hear it. The only way he gets a voice at the table is if he authentically and strategically engages his craft in his mission field.

How could this look for you? Where has God placed you that you might be running from?

Maybe it's as simple as redeeming the seemingly mundane tasks, such as schoolwork or cooking or a part-time job, and God is so pleased when we do this.

Or maybe it's figuring out exactly what those desires are in our hearts—art, drawing, writing—and creating to the best of our abilities. We know God delights in us when this happens.

And here's the awesome part: All the stuff we create doesn't just go up in smoke. Some of it will because it's created with the wrong intent or heart, but we aren't here to just work and have it count for nothing. It will be a part of the fully restored and redeemed city of God. God's working to build his church and looking to make that city; all he asks is if we want in.[16]

1. How does caring for the earth show love to God? What are some practical ways you can do this?
2. Why is it difficult to see God's image in other people and treat them with dignity?
3. Do you label things as *sacred* or *secular*? Why or why not?
4. Why do we often forget to give God the glory when it comes to the things of everyday life, such as food and music?
5. How can you be used for God's glory in your current situation?
6. All truth is God's truth. Are you willing to accept it even if it comes from unexpected sources? Why or why not?
7. How can the Christian subculture in art and music be redeemed?

# CHAPTER 10

# WHY JESUS LOVES THE CHURCH (AND YOU SHOULD TOO)

At the moment of me writing this I've been married a little over four months. Looking back on my big wedding day, I'd be kidding myself to say I wasn't more excited than I'd been in my entire life. I got to marry the woman of my dreams. What is better than that?

I remember the week of the wedding I kept wondering if I was going to cry the minute the doors opened and I saw her walking down the aisle toward me. If my crying as an attendee of previous weddings was any indication, then it was pretty safe to say what the outcome would be. What can I say, I'm a softie.

During that craze leading up to the wedding, I thought

deeply about marriage—the vows and promises, the ceremony and reception.

The elation, the waiting, the coming together as one.

Think about it: There is nothing more descriptive of our relationship with Jesus than marriage. No wonder Jesus calls the church his bride.

The same feelings I felt on my wedding day are only a shadow of Jesus' feelings toward his bride, the church. Can you imagine how beautiful that day will be?

All the tears.

All the messy corridors of life.

All the mountaintops.

They culminate in that moment.

The romancing, the wooing, the calling—finally collide with completion.

The past fades to black.

The doors open.

The music plays.

And Jesus watches us walk down the aisle to him. Clothed in white, his perfect righteousness.

That is the beauty of marriage. Every time you go to a wedding, you are seeing something deeply reflective of something else. The splendor and beauty are just shadows, a mist of what is to come for those who trust in Jesus. At every single wedding, Jesus is pulling back the curtain on eternity and whispering, "That's me and you!"

## MORE THAN STALE CRACKERS AND GRAPE JUICE

I see so much beauty in the church now, but when I was younger, I saw it differently. My mom and I attended frequently, but I would not have called myself a "church kid." I didn't get enough gold stars. Church to me was where kids went to die from boredom. I didn't see what was so spectacular about stale crackers and tiny amounts of grape juice. In high school, I still went occasionally for the girls but finally stopped going altogether. It just seemed so outdated. Disconnected. I didn't see the point in going anymore.

It wasn't until I understood what church is supposed to be that I developed a deep love for my brothers and sisters in the faith. The Greek word for *church* is *ekklesia*, which means a "people called out."[1] What I love about that definition is it has nothing to do with a building. Church in America is viewed as a brick building with a cross on top. Church in the New Testament is a group of people with the power of Jesus in them unleashing grace on anyone and everyone they encounter.

That means when you leave "church" on Sundays, the church is leaving.

The church isn't a building; it's people.

The church isn't a dead club; it's a living organism.

When I started to see this, I still felt some hesitancy. It was furthered by the first church I strolled into after I started to follow Jesus. I went there for a decent amount of time but never felt part of a family. I was just a number. Also I struggled because I seemed different from everyone else. Week after week the pastor would call someone on stage to share a *testimony*, which is just the Christian word for "life story." The person would walk up and usually say something to this effect: "Hi, my name is John. I was an alcoholic and a porn addict for forty years. Then Jesus saved me, and I've never thought about a drop of alcohol since. Now to fill my days I listen to praise and worship music while interceding for the nations twenty-four hours a day."

I remember wondering what *interceding* meant.

I heard this story week after week. Every time someone told it, I remember slipping a little lower in my chair and wondering if there was something wrong with me. *How come I still struggle with lust? How come I still have the desire to do some of those things I don't want to do anymore? If I don't have that testimony, does that mean I'm not saved? Did I not do it right?*

These questions would swirl and swirl and push me deeper into secrecy. By the looks of it, I couldn't be honest. I couldn't struggle. I couldn't be transparent. I almost stopped going to church altogether. It just didn't seem like it was for me. I was trying to be something I wasn't.

That's when I experienced the real church. I had just started meeting with one of my former high school teachers. I knew he was a Christian when I took his class, so when I started to follow Jesus, I reached out to him. He is one of the manliest men I know. He was an NCAA national champion wrestler. His biceps are the size of my head. Even in high school, he commanded tons of respect. I remember admiring him and looking up to his work ethic, integrity, and discipline.

When I first began meeting with him, I was a little intimidated. At the same time, Jesus began to persistently nudge me to be honest, be transparent, and stop hiding. I still remember breaking down and coming clean. Sharing with him my struggles, my guilt, my shame, and my baggage.

There's something really scary in moments like that because you never know how someone will react. When you take the mask off, you run the risk of being rejected. And not just rejected for your fake self, but being rejected for your vulnerable self.

In that moment, my former biology teacher looked me straight in the eye and revealed how he shared those same struggles. How he had difficulties similar to mine at certain points in his life and how he experienced God's grace in those moments. He didn't bat an eye or pause for a second. He seemed used to being that transparent and open.

At first I was shocked. I remember thinking, *You're not*

*allowed to say that. You're the big macho Christian man. You're the leader. You can't show weakness.* But it was in that moment I first saw the church being the church. God used that example and many similar ones down the road to show me the church wasn't a place to act good but a place to drop the act.

The church is a place to be transparent and
vulnerable.
The church is a place to take off the mask.
The church is a place you can be yourself.

I saw that the church wasn't a museum for good people; it was a hospital for the broken. Jesus wasn't trying to create a place to show off his shiny employees; he wanted a place where his children could be healed.

## THE BODY OF JESUS

Remember when you first met the person closest to you? Maybe it was a spouse, a friend, a sibling, a parent, whoever. Just think for a minute about the beginning stage of that relationship. How did you get to know that person? Did you meet them randomly? Did you talk over coffee? What events collided to actually weave your lives together? When did you get to the point of actually feeling like you knew that person?

I can still remember this with Alyssa. It wasn't just one big event but rather a lot of small events that led us closer and closer together. Bonfires. Trips to Chipotle. Church. Talks on the phone. Whenever she told me something about herself, I wouldn't stop there. I kept asking. I kept pursuing. To this day, I am still getting to know her.

But imagine what would have happened if, when I met Alyssa, I only focused on one part of her. Would she feel known? Even more so, imagine how awkward it would be if I only focused on one part of her, like, say, her toe. What if when I was trying to get to know Alyssa, I just stared at her toe? Talked to her toe? Listened to her toe?

First of all, if you ever see me doing that, call the cops. Second, would that give me a proper picture of who she is? Of course not.

Consider what the apostle Paul told the church of Corinth:

For the body does not consist of one member but of many. If the foot should say, "Because I am not a hand, I do not belong to the body," that would not make it any less a part of the body. And if the ear should say, "Because I am not an eye, I do not belong to the body," that would not make it any less a part of the body. If the whole body were an eye, where would be the sense of hearing? If the whole body were an ear, where would be the sense of smell? But as it is, God arranged the members in the body, each one of them, as he chose. If all were a single member, where would the body be? As it is, there are many parts, yet one body.[2]

Paul makes it clear that when we become Christians, we become a part of Jesus' body. He has wrapped us in himself. His mission with the church is for it to become his body. We aren't representing ourselves; we are representing Jesus. This also means that Christianity isn't as individualistic as some make us think. While it's intensely personal, it's not private. After trusting in Jesus, we are immediately joined together in something greater.

If the church is Jesus' body, then to know who Jesus is, I need to know the church. In the same way staring at Alyssa's toe in order to get to know her is ridiculous and inadequate, so it is with looking at one individual or part of the body of Christ to get a good picture of who Jesus is. In fact, if we just stare at the toe, we will probably get a really poor picture of who he is! Toes are messy and gross—just as we are messy as individuals. But all of us together make up a picture of Jesus.

Different functions.
Different gifts.
Different jobs.

We can't say we love Jesus and not the church because that's like cutting off someone's body and saying you love a decapitated head. That's gross. And it's weird. To love someone and know that person fully, you must know *their entire self.*

Zooming in on a leg or an arm or a particular muscle will give you a distorted view of who God is and what he is doing today. But if you zoom out and become part of the larger picture, then you'll see the true Jesus.

One of the things I love to do is to people watch. I always feel like a sociologist just staring, watching, and studying. Sometimes when I visit churches, it feels more like a VIP access club than a place where all nations, tongues, races, and ages collide. And I find it sad when the DMV, post office, and airport have more diversity than the church of God commissioned by God to go make disciples of all nations.

But I've also been privileged to see the church at its best. When you see it, you know it and it's a beautiful thing. I've seen a seventy-five-year-old upper-class, suspender-wearing businessman shouting praise songs to Jesus right next to a sixteen-year-old saggy-pants-wearing teen with a backward hat doing the same thing.

Both worshiping Jesus.
Both a part of the church.
Both glorifying God.

That is what the church is supposed to be.

It has to be church when the only thing that is bringing diverse people into the same room is their love for Jesus. Not their jobs. Not their socioeconomic statuses. Not their races. But their mutual love for Jesus. That's when you know it's the church.

If everyone in your church talks like you, acts like you,

and dresses like you, Jesus may not be the one you're worshiping. It may be you. Nothing would be weirder than a bunch of hands severed from the body and gathered in a particular place—unless it's an episode of *The Addams Family*. It should look just as weird when we call ourselves a church but are just a bunch of clones. That's not a church; that's a club.

Instead of attending church for a certain type of music or a particular teacher or because they serve good coffee, we should be attending church based on our common love for Jesus. He should be the real reason we gather together and more importantly live life together. That's what makes us family. Otherwise it just doesn't work because those other reasons can go away.

## A PLACE OF STRENGTH

For me, the best part about the church is that God has uniquely wired it as his vehicle to heal and offer grace to hurting people. The church is a shelter from the storms.

There have been times when my sin and guilt and shame have so overtaken me, I felt like I couldn't go another day. It was in those moments the church became a place of strength, similar to a tree in a storm. If one tree is standing alone and a storm comes, that tree could be knocked down and uprooted. But if there are thousands of trees standing together in a forest, they all lean with the wind and take the force together, spreading out the winds evenly. That is what the church is supposed to do—bear one another's burdens, pray for one another, and confess sins to one another.

When we look at the church this way, we see its failures differently. A lot of people like to sit on the outside, call it a place full of hypocrites, and throw their sins in the church's face. But some like to roll up their sleeves and realize they are a part of the problem. When we start following Jesus, we become members of Jesus' bride. That means when there is a problem in his body—the church—we lend our part of the body to the healing process.

How stupid would it look if when someone broke a hand, the foot started criticizing the hand? That's what we look like when we Christians begin to criticize the church. One part of the body should lend itself to the healing process of another hurting member.

That's love.

That's the gospel.

And that is Jesus.

The difference between a critic and a servant is how they approach a problem. A critic stands back and points out the problem; a servant rolls up his or her sleeves and helps *solve* the problem. The worst part is when the criticism comes from within the same body. A lot of Christians like to lob grenades at one another rather than bear one another's burdens in love. We often don't realize the damage we are causing.

When Christ's body is divided, who bleeds?

Jesus.

When Christians fight among themselves, Jesus is the one whose reputation is damaged and bruised. Imagine the pain, blood, and damage if an arm divided itself. That's what it's like when Christians fight each other.

But when the church is being the church, it is a family atmosphere and a place of safety. A place where we help heal each other's hurt and grief. A place of strength.

## THE CHURCH IN THE CITY

I've grown up in the Northwest. Born and raised right outside of Seattle, I went to school near Portland. It's definitely a place where a good chunk of the society is disillusioned with church. Some people even move there to get away from a religious atmosphere.

Too many people in the Northwest have been told about Jesus but have never been shown Jesus. It would be ludicrous to say we don't ever need to tell people about Jesus, but I am saying sometimes we can show the unique power of grace to build bridges and tear down walls.

Right after the financial collapse of 2008, Portland took a major hit, as did other large cities around the nation. People were struggling economically, educationally, and socially. A few predominant churches in the area, including Imago Dei and Solid Rock, saw the need and wanted to fill in the gap.

They got together and approached the openly gay mayor of Portland, Sam Adams. At first he was skeptical. "Would this be about missionary work? Could a liberal city like Portland pull it off?" But the church leaders promised the mission was simply to serve the needs of the city.

This reminds me of what the prophet Jeremiah wrote to Israel: "But seek the welfare of the city where I have sent you into exile, and pray to the LORD on its behalf, for in its welfare you will find your welfare."[3] Isn't that crazy? God actually called the Israelites to seek the welfare of a city where they had been sent as punishment. He called them to pray for the city on its behalf. Sounds like God cares a lot more than we do.

Back in Portland, churches agreed to serve and not evangelize. Agreeing to serve without preaching, the churches did exactly that. In today's culture we have to be creative and look for ways to meet basic needs and share Jesus. It's not one or the other. Social justice isn't pitted against gospel proclamation. Jesus called us to do both, so let's start.

The mayor of Portland skeptically agreed to let the churches help serve. They asked what were the greatest needs of the city, and he quickly noted hunger, homelessness, environment, schools, and others.

So what did the churches do? They rolled up their sleeves and got their hands dirty. They sent twenty-six thousand volunteers to work on service projects in each of the main areas of concern. They established SOS (Season of Service) where they serve, regularly showing the compassion, love, and redemption of Jesus corporately. The churches saw it as a beautiful opportunity to live out the already-laid-out job description of the church—being his hands and feet. I can't imagine how many non-Christians saw this at first and had no idea what to think.

Ken Weigel of Imago Dei, one of the Portland churches involved, said it best when speaking about their motivation: "We wanted to bless the city. We wanted the city to miss the church if we were to leave."

Is that true of you? Your church? Your city?

If a meteor hit your church community, would anyone notice or care? And if they did care, would it be out of concern or thankfulness "that church" is gone? We ought to take a hard look at ourselves in our communities and ask if we are truly joining in what Jesus is already doing. When asked about who should get the credit for the Portland churches stepping up, Ken Weigel said, "Jesus showed up long before we got there. Christ is unveiling his kingdom all over Portland. I'm just joining with him."[4]

And in those moments, the church becomes beautiful.

## BROKEN EDGES BECOME BEAUTIFUL

In the New Testament, the church was seen as completely radical in its time:

Poor and rich people didn't mingle in society, but
they did in the church.

Gentiles and Jews wouldn't associate in society, but
they did in the church.
Men and women weren't equal in society, but they
were in the church.

That's the church Jesus came to bring, and that's the
church we are a part of if we have trusted him. All racial, societal, political, and financial walls were abolished. We are all
one in Jesus.

This is what church is supposed to look like. I know it's
not perfect, but don't let a bad experience hold you back
from healing. Don't let it hold you back from Jesus. Give it
another chance. Just because someone wore a cross around
his neck or had one at the top of the brick building doesn't
mean you witnessed a church. You'll know the true church
when you see it. They are a peculiar people called out of the
world but sent into the world to be agents of reconciliation
to the world.

At the deepest level we all have an incredible desire to just
be known.

To just be accepted.

To just be loved.

It calls us. It beckons us. It whispers to us.

It offers that place.

Come to Jesus, and then come to his body. Trying to live
without community is like trying to live without oxygen.
We weren't created to do it. I know from experience there is

nothing more freeing than being able to gather regularly with people who see me without the mask.

Without the hiding.

Without the act.

We all come in with baggage.

We all come in trying to find our way.

We all come in with broken edges.

In the same way a mosaic is made up of broken, ragged, and dirty pieces of glass, so the church is made up of broken, ragged, and dirty people. But when you zoom out and see the whole picture, you see something beautiful.

Broken people living life together is a beautiful picture.

1. Does thinking of the church as a living organism rather than a building challenge your understanding of it? Why or why not?

2. How can Christians create an environmont that promotes more transparency and authenticity rather than less?

3. When we follow Jesus, we become part of something much larger: Christ's body, the church. Is it easier for you to be solitary in your faith or to be a part of a diverse community? Explain your response.

4. Have you encountered the church as a place of healing? Explain why or why not.

5. Describe the church at its best the way you understand it. What does it look like, who is there, and how are you serving others?

6. How can you deepen your relationship with Jesus and choose to follow him as he is portrayed in the Gospels, and not as so-called religious folks present him?

# CONCLUSION

*Do You Know Jesus?*

The process of writing this book has been crazy. It has eas-ily been the biggest project I've ever undertaken. Some days I blazed through the writing, but other days I just stared at my thirteen-inch Macbook Pro's screen not ever pressing one button. All in all the process has been rewarding as I have fleshed out what I believe, written it in a way that articulates my heart, and hopefully helped at least one reader.

Over and over again I'd start to stress or feel inadequate about writing this book. It would be two o'clock in the morn-ing as the coffee was starting to fade, and I'd wonder, *Am I really doing this? What if no one reads it?* In those moments I remembered my one goal: to do everything in my power to talk about Jesus to as many people as possible. I wrote this hoping one person out there might read my feeble narrative and come closer to Jesus. Then it would be worth it.

Maybe she'd give Jesus another chance.

Maybe he'd investigate Jesus a little more.

Maybe you'd rethink your current worldview.

That was—and is—my hope.

So reading this finished book and remembering all the time, energy, and coffee that went into making it happen, I hope you are now hearing Jesus whisper in the depths of your soul that he is better than anything you've ever imagined. Or I hope that if you know someone who is asking questions that you'll pass along this book.

If you are reading this book and feel that tug, but you wonder where to begin, then you're not alone. I struggled with that same question when Jesus first started drawing me toward him. Relax; you don't have to have it all figured out. All you need to do is come to him. If you're thinking, *I have nothing to give or nothing to offer Jesus right now*, that's exactly where he wants you. He just wants dependency; he just wants you. You don't have to clean yourself up to come to Jesus. You come to Jesus, and he cleans you up.

I can't imagine what you are going through right now—trials, suffering, heartache, pain. But I can tell you that whatever it is, it's not too big for God. His grace can cover it, and your heart can be made new. In those times when I felt like I was drowning, I thought God was off in a distant land. Later I realized that's when he is most near.

He's near you too.

I heard a story awhile back about some friends who went swimming in a river. It was spring, and the glacier runoff had made the river pretty dangerous. Nonetheless one of the guys jumped in, got caught in the current, and was taken to the dangerous part of the rapids. One of his friends on the shore was a lifeguard, and all the other friends looked at him to do something. He just stood there, though, not moving, just staring at his friend. The others began to panic and yell at him and tell him to go save his friend! Still nothing. They looked out into the river and saw their friend struggling desperately. In an instant, though, the struggle stopped. He could no longer fight and began to drown. When that happened, the lifeguard jumped in and with a few swift strokes rescued the friend and brought him to shore.

With the adrenaline wearing off, the group yelled at the lifeguard, "Why didn't you jump in earlier? He could've died!"

He calmly looked at them and said, "I had to wait until he fully gave up. Unless he stopped fighting, he would have dragged me under and drowned me with him. But the minute he gave up, I could save him."

That's what it's like with Jesus. He just wants us to surrender, and when we do, he comes and gets us. The waves might be crashing overhead, but in that moment, when it looks like we might die, his grace scoops us up and brings us life. And because we finally give up, we know it was him who did all the saving.

Will you surrender? I don't know where you are or where

you're coming from, but I know Jesus has a better plan for your life than you do. He is a better king of your life than you are. No one has caused me more hurt, shame, guilt, and pain than me. He knows, and he rescues me. He can do the same for you. Just come as you are.

Are you tired? Worn out? Burned out on religion? Come to me. Get away with me and you'll recover your life. I'll show you how to take a real rest. Walk with me and work with me—watch how I do it. Learn the unforced rhythms of grace. I won't lay anything heavy or ill-fitting on you. Keep company with me and you'll learn to live freely and lightly.[1]

I'd love to keep in contact with you and
hear your feedback on the book!

 : twitter.com/jeffersonbethke

 : facebook.com/jeffersonbethkepage

 : youtube.com/bball1989

# ACKNOWLEDGMENTS

To Alyssa: My beautiful and amazing love of my life. This book seriously wouldn't have been possible without your constant encouragement, inspiration, and sacrifice. I'm still humbled you married me, and I'm thankful we get to walk this journey of life together.

To my family: Thank you for always being there! I know that no matter what happens, I always have you all. Thank you for teaching me how to love, live, and serve.

To Sealy, Curtis, and Matt: Thanks for believing in me! Without you guys giving me a shot, this book wouldn't be possible. Your guidance, advice, and grace have been invaluable.

To Steve: Thanks for being such a great mentor. I've learned how to love, laugh, and pursue Jesus more deeply because of you.

To Jeff: Thanks for being such a great friend this past year. Road trips, red-eye flights, media interviews—I couldn't have stayed sane without you!

To Matt: Thanks for wanting to make a video of that initial poem. It's been fun to ride the wave with you and continue to make quality videos we both care about!

To Angela: Thanks for so much help in the writing process! Your expertise was truly a gift. This book would be a far cry from what it is now without you. It was a joy to work with you!

To Thomas Nelson: Thanks for believing in this book enough to publish it! The team has been nothing but gracious and helpful.

# NOTES

*Introduction: Why I Hate Religion but Love Jesus*
   1. 1 Corinthians 1:27.

*Chapter 1: Will the Real Jesus Please Stand Up?*
   1. C. S. Lewis, *The Problem of Pain*, in *The Complete C. S. Lewis* (San Francisco: HarperCollins, 2002), 406.
   2. 2 Timothy 3:12.
   3. Matthew 23.
   4. John 2:1–11, 13–22; 4:1–42; 5:18, 19–29; 6:53.
   5. John 8:1–11.
   6. "Holiday Spending Sized Up," *IBIS World*, Special Report August 2010, http://www.ibisworld.com/Common /MediaCenter/Holiday%20Spending.pdf (accessed January 23, 2013).
   7. "Holy Pancake Auctioned on eBay: Woman Says Jesus Appeared on Breakfast," WPBF News, November 13, 2007, http://www.wpbf.com/Holy-Pancake-Auctioned-On-eBay/-/8789538/5117954/-/item/0/-/wwodsaz/-/index.html (accessed January 23, 2013).

8. C. S. Lewis, *The Lion, the Witch and the Wardrobe: A Story for Children* (1950; repr., New York: HarperCollins, 2009), 77.

9. Isaiah 40:31; Jeremiah 29:11.

10. Revelation 19:15–16.

11. Matthew 16:24.

12. Isaiah 64:6 NIV.

13. Francis Chan, *Crazy Love: Overwhelmed by a Relentless God* (Colorado Springs: David C. Cook, 2008), 58.

14. Matthew 23.

15. Matthew 21:31–32.

16. 1 Samuel 16:7.

*Chapter 2: Why I Still Think Jesus Hates Religion (and You Should Too)*

1. D. L. Moody, *The Gospel Awakening: Comprising the Sermons and Addresses of the Great Revival Meetings Conducted by Moody and Sankey*, ed. L. T. Remlap, 16th ed. (Chicago: F. H. Revell, 1883), 690.

2. Matthew 5:17–18.

3. Hebrews 10.

4. *Dietrich Bonhoeffer Works*, ed. Eberhard Bethge, trans. Reginald H. Fuller, vol. 8, *Letters and Papers From Prison* (Minneapolis: Ausberg Fortress, 2009), 362.

5. Matthew 5:17.

*Chapter 3: Fundies, Fakes, and Other So-Called Christians*

1. Mark 8:34–35.

2. John 2:1–11.

3. Matthew 23:23.

4. Matthew 22:1–14; Luke 15:22–23.

5. Galatians 5:11–12.

6. Brennan Manning, *The Ragamuffin Gospel* (1990; repr., Sisters, OR: Multnomah, 2005), 199.

7. Luke 15:11–32.

8. Luke 15:2.

9. Luke 15:25.
10. Luke 15:28.
11. Luke 15:29–30.
12. Luke 15:23–24.
13. Luke 15:31–32.

*Chapter 4: Religion Makes Enemies / Jesus Makes Friends*

1. "Boston Police Accept 'Full Responsibility' in Death of Red
   Sox Fan," CNN.us, October 22, 2004, http://articles.cnn
   .com/2004-10-22/us/fan.death_1_victoria-snelgrove-police
   -commissioner-kathleen-o-toole-dreadful-irony?_s=PM:US
   (accessed January 29, 2013); "Brutal Yankees–Red Sox Fan
   Fight Caught on Video at Yankee Stadium," CBS New York,
   April 30, 2012, http://newyork.cbslocal.com/2012/04/30
   /brutal-yankees-red-sox-fan-fight-caught-on-tape-at-yankee
   -stadium/ (accessed January 29, 2012).
2. John 17:21.
3. Richard Overy, *The Dictators: Hitler's Germany and Stalin's
   Russia* (New York: W. W. Norton, 2004), 265–303.
4. Colossians 3:5.
5. Matthew 5:44.
6. Nik Ripkin, *The Insanity of God: A True Story of Faith
   Resurrected* (Nashville: B & H Books, 2013).
7. In 1 Corinthians 5:9–13, Paul tells the Corinthian church to
   "Purge the evil person from among you." He is specifically
   referring to self-professed Christians openly engaging in
   sexual immorality, although greed, idolatry, drunkenness,
   and other socially offensive sins are mentioned as well. As
   professed Christians, we are supposed to separate corporately
   from other believers who are publicly engaging in sin—but
   that doesn't mean we shouldn't continue to meet, pursue,
   and give grace to those believers individually. It also doesn't
   mean that we should shun the sinning nonbeliever. As Paul
   says, "God judges those outside [the church]." We don't. As

Christians, we are to show God's grace to the nonbelieving
world so they, too, may fall in love with him.
8. 1 Corinthians 6:9–11.
9. Romans 8:37; 2 Corinthians 12:7.
10. Hebrews 12:1–2.
11. John 4:1–24.
12. Bill Maher, "New Rules," *Real Time with Bill Maher*, 213,
    HBO, May 13, 2011, http://www.hbo.com/real-time-with
    -bill-maher/episodes/0/213-episode/article/new-rules.html
    (accessed January 29, 2013).

*Chapter 5: With Religion, There Are Good and Bad People /
With Jesus, There Are Only Bad People in Need of Grace*
1. Matthew 5:27–28.
2. Matthew 5:20.
3. Genesis 6:5–6.
4. Genesis 19:30–38; 2 Samuel 13; Judges 19:29–30.
5. John 5:39–40.
6. Jonah 1.
7. Genesis 4:1–16.
8. 1 Samuel 17.

*Chapter 6: Religion Is the Means to Get Things from
God / If We Seek Jesus, We Get God*
1. Mark 10:17–27.
2. 2 Corinthians 8:9.
3. Ephesians 1:3.
4. 3 John 2.
5. Genesis 2:15.
6. C. S. Lewis to Dom Bede Griffiths, 23 April 1951 in *The
    Collected Letters of C. S. Lewis*, ed. Walter Hooper, vol.
    3, *Narnia, Cambridge, and Joy 1950–1963* (New York:
    HarperCollins, 2007), 111.

7. 1 Peter 3:18.
8. Augustine of Hippo, *Augustine Confessions: Books I–IV*, ed. Gillian Clark (Cambridge: Cambridge University, 1995), 84.
9. Ripkin, *The Insanity of God*, 154.
10. Ibid., x.
11. Ephesians 1:3.
12. Colossians 3:3–4.

Chapter 7: With Religion, If You Are Suffering, God Is Punishing You / God Already Punished Jesus on Your Behalf, So Suffering Is His Mercy

1. Genesis 50:20.
2. Elisabeth Kübler-Ross, *Death: The Final Stage of Growth* (New York: Touchstone, 1986), 96.
3. Hebrews 13:5.
4. Isaiah 53:3–5.
5. Psalm 68:5.
6. Psalm 147:3.
7. Rob Bell, *Sex God: Exploring the Endless Connections Between Sexuality and Spirituality* (2007; New York: HarperOne, 2012), 98.
8. Romans 12:19.
9. Hebrews 11:1.
10. Revelation 21:1.
11. Revelation 21:3–5.

Chapter 8: Religion Says, "God Will Love You If . . ." / Jesus Says, "God So Loved . . ."

1. Hebrews 12:1–2.
2. Robert Robinson, "Come, Thou Fount of Every Blessing," in *A Collection of Hymns Used by the Church of Christ in Angel Alley* (Bishopsgate, 1759).
3. Romans 4:5.
4. Hebrews 4:11.

5. Jefferson Bethke, "Sexual Healing," http://youtu.be /IlJFvxad1_A (accessed January 30, 2013).
6. John 8:1–11.
7. Leviticus 20:10; Deuteronomy 22:22.
8. Romans 5:20.
9. Hosea 1:2.
10. Hosea 3:2.
11. See Luke 15:4–10.
12. See Exodus 20:5.
13. Luke 15:18–19.
14. Luke 15:21.
15. Luke 15:22–24.
16. Steve Brown, "Lincoln at the Slave Block," *Men of Integrity*, ChristianityToday.com, January 21, 2000, http://www .christianitytoday.com/moi/2000/001/january/lincoln-at -slave-block.html (accessed January 31, 2012).
17. Homer, *The Odyssey: The Story of Odysseus*, trans. W. H. D. Rouse (New York: Penguin, 1999), 138–142.
18. Apollonius Rhodius, *The Argonautica*, trans. R. C. Seaton (New York: Macmillan, 1912), 355–357.

*Chapter 9: Religion Points to a Dim Future / Jesus Points to a Bright Future*
1. Romans 8:20–22.
2. Genesis 1:26.
3. 1 Timothy 4:4–5.
4. 1 Corinthians 10:31.
5. 2 Corinthians 5:18.
6. John 4:19–24.
7. R. Jamieson, A. R. Fausset, and D. Brown, *Commentary Critical and Explanatory on the Whole Bible*, Acts 17:28 (Oak Harbor, WA: Logos Research Systems, 1997).
8. Romans 11:36.

9. Acts 17:16.

10. John 4:24.

11. Matthew 16:18.

12. 2 Corinthians 5:20.

13. Psalm 37:4.

14. *The Works of Saint Augustine: A Translation for the 21st Century*, trans. Augustinian Heritage Institute, *Homilies on the First Epistle of John*, vol. 14 (New York: New City, 2008), 110.

15. John MacArthur, "Delight Yourself in the Lord (and Do Whatever You Want!)," *Grace to You*, December 21, 2010, http://www.gty.org/blog/B101221 (accessed January 31, 2013).

16. 1 Corinthians 3; Revelation 21:1–8.

*Chapter 10: Why Jesus Loves the Church (and You Should Too)*

1. A. C. Myers, *The Eerdmans Bible Dictionary* (Grand Rapids, MI: Eerdmans, 1987), 215.

2. 1 Corinthians 12:14–20.

3. Jeremiah 29:7.

4. Presentation, Q Conference, Portland, Oregon, April 2011.

*Conclusion: Do You Know Jesus?*

1. Matthew 11:28–30 MSG.

# RECOMMENDED READING

Since I am a self-professed book geek, I wanted to include some of the books that helped me in my Christian journey, in case they may help you too. Much of what I wrote in this book just touches the surface, but there are many other authors who have dedicated their lives to studying these topics. These are a few of my favorites:

*Chapter 1: Will the Real Jesus Please Stand Up?*

*Vintage Jesus* by Mark Driscoll and Gerry Breshears (Crossway, 2008)

*Mere Christianity* by C. S. Lewis (Harper Collins, 1952)

*Who Is This Man?* by John Ortberg (Zondervan, 2012)

*Jesus + Nothing = Everything* by Tullian Tchividjian (Crossway, 2011)

*Your Jesus Is Too Safe* by Jared Wilson (Kregal, 2009)

*Why Jesus?* by Ravi Zacharias (Faith Words, 2012)

*Chapter 2: Why I Still Think Jesus Hates Religion (and You Should Too)*

Cost of Discipleship by Dietrich Bonhoeffer (MacMillan, 1959)
Letters and Papers from Prison by Dietrich Bonhoeffer
   (Touchstone, 1997)
The Ragamuffin Gospel by Brennan Manning (Multnomah, 2005)
Bonhoeffer by Eric Metaxas (Thomas Nelson, 2010)
The Normal Christian Life by Watchman Nee (Wilder, 2008)
The Pursuit of God by A. W. Tozer (Christian Publications, 1948)

*Chapter 3: Fundies, Fakes, and Other So-Called Christians*

Not a Fan by Kyle Idleman (Zondervan, 2011)
The Prodigal God by Timothy Keller (Penguin, 2008)
Radical by David Platt (Multnomah, 2010)

*Chapter 4: Religion Makes Enemies / Jesus Makes Friends*

Love Does by Bob Goff (Thomas Nelson, 2012)
The Mortification of Sin by John Owen (Trinity, 2012)

*Chapter 5: With Religion, There Are Good and Bad People /
With Jesus, There Are Only Bad People in Need of Grace*

Three Free Sins by Steve Brown (Howard, 2012)
The Reason for God by Timothy Keller (Penguin, 2008)
How Good Is Good Enough? by Andy Stanley (Multnomah, 2008)

*Chapter 6: Religion Is the Means to Get Things from
God / If We Seek Jesus, We Get God*

The Practice of the Presence of God by Brother Lawrence (Revell,
   1958)
God Is the Gospel by John Piper (Crossway, 2005)
The Heavenly Man by Brother Yun (Lion Hudson, 2002)

*Chapter 7: With Religion, If You Are Suffering, God Is Punishing You / God Already Punished Jesus on Your Behalf, So Suffering Is His Mercy*

The Goodness of God by Randy Alcorn (Multnomah, 2010)

If God Is Good by Randy Alcorn (Multnomah, 2009)

How Long, O Lord? by D. A. Carson (Baker, 1990)

Death by Love by Mark Driscoll and Gerry Breshears (Crossway, 2008)

When the Darkness Will Not Lift by John Piper (Crossway, 2006)

The Insanity of God by Nik Ripken (B & H Books, 2013)

The Bruised Reed by Richard Sibbes (Empire Books, 2011)

*Chapter 8: Religion Says, "God Will Love You If . . ." / Jesus Says, "God So Loved . . ."*

Grace and Truth Paradox by Randy Alcorn (Multnomah, 2003)

Transforming Grace by Jerry Bridges (NavPress, 1991)

Crazy Love by Francis Chan (Cook, 2008)

The Explicit Gospel by Matt Chandler (Crossway, 2012)

King's Cross by Timothy Keller (Penguin, 2011)

The Meaning of Marriage by Timothy Keller (Penguin, 2011)

Commentary on Galatians by Martin Luther (Classic Books, 2009)

When Godly People Do Ungodly Things by Beth Moore (B & H Books, 2002)

Redeeming Love by Francine Rivers (Multnomah, 2007)

All of Grace by Charles Spurgeon (Moody, 2010)

The Grace of God by Andy Stanley (Thomas Nelson, 2010)

The Grace Awakening by Charles Swindoll (Thomas Nelson, 1990)

*Chapter 9: Religion Points to a Dim Future / Jesus Points to a Bright Future*

Heaven by Randy Alcorn (Tyndale, 2004)

How Now Shall We Live? by Charles Colson and Nancy Pearcey (Tyndale, 1999)

Culture Making by Andy Crouch (InterVarsity, 2008)

Dug Down Deep by Joshua Harris (Multnomah, 2010)

*Total Truth* by Nancy Pearcey (Crossway, 2005)
*Art for God's Sake* by Philip Ryken (P and R Publishing, 2006)
*Art and the Bible* by Francis Schaeffer (InterVarsity, 2010)
*How Should We Then Live?* by Francis Schaeffer (Revell, 1976)
*Imagine* by Steve Turner (InterVarsity, 2001)

### Chapter 10: Why Jesus Loves the Church (and You Should Too)

*Community* by Brad House (Crossway, 2011)
*Center Church* by Timothy Keller (Zondervan, 2012)
*Generous Justice* by Timothy Keller (Penguin, 2010)
*Surprised by Hope* by N. T. Wright (HarperOne, 2008)

# ABOUT THE AUTHOR

Hey everyone!

If you made it this far in the book then I owe you a huge thank you. The culture of book reading is a peculiar thing where you feel like you are getting to know someone—agreeing with them, disagreeing with them, laughing, crying, and dialoguing with them along the way. The only bummer about that process, though, is it's a one-way street. My hope in writing the book is to put it in your hands and hopefully walk this journey together, but the thing I dislike about book writing is that I don't get to hear *your* story, *your* journey, and *your* end of the dialogue.

So I thought I'd go first to take away the awkwardness. As you read, because I couldn't help but mention her dozens of times, I'm married to my amazing wife Alyssa. We live near Tacoma, Washington, with our yellow lab puppy named Aslan (I'm a big Narnia fan). I also am a cofounder of a recent social entrepreneur startup called Claro Candles where we raise funds and awareness for causes people care about by selling quality candles in hopes to bring light to social injustice. During a typical week I usually try to make something creative (poems, videos, writing, etc.) and I help out with a college ministry in town. During our free time Alyssa and I like to read and watch old TV shows on Netflix.

Well, that's me I guess (hopefully not all of it!). Would love to hear your story, as it pertains to this book or just in general. My contact info is below. Feel free to ask, critique, question, or just say hello. Appreciate you!

Twitter: www.twitter.com/jeffersonbethke
Instagram: www.instagram.com/jeffersonbethke
Pinterest: www.pinterest.com/jeffersonbethke
Facebook: www.facebook.com/jeffersonbethkepage
Youtube: www.youtube.com/bball1989

# KEEP IN TOUCH WITH WHAT IS GOING ON WITH JESUS > RELIGION AND JEFFERSON BETHKE!

Visit jesusisgreater.tv for more updates, news, videos, and giveaways.

JesusIsGreater.tv